OPIUM REDUCTION IN THAILAND 1970–2000

A THIRTY-YEAR JOURNEY

D0148912

OPIUM REDUCTION IN THAILAND
1970–2000
A THIRTY-YEAR JOURNEY

Prepared by

RONALD D. RENARD

for the

United Nations International Drug Control Programme
Regional Centre for East Asia and the Pacific
Bangkok, Thailand

UNDCP

SILKWORM BOOKS

ISBN 974-88553-6-8

First published in 2001 by
Silkworm Books
104/5 Chiang Mai–Hot Road, M. 7, Chiang Mai 50200, Thailand
E-mail: silkworm@loxinfo.co.th

Cover photographs: TG-HDP, UNDCP
Set in 12 pt. Garamond by Silk Type

Printed by O. S. Printing House, Bangkok

CONTENTS

I BACKGROUND

II PROCESS

CONTENTS

III ANALYSIS

LIST OF TABLES AND FIGURES

TABLES

FIGURES

FOREWORD

A journey towards freedom from opium.

Hundreds of thousands of people were involved in this thirty-year journey in Thailand.

A large number of governments and their taxpayers helped with significant foreign aid.

Hundreds of experts from Thailand and other countries spent years leading and facilitating a complex process of change.

Impressive results have been achieved. Those who are skeptical might wish to spend a few days with villagers of the Doi Tung project.

Very soon the Hall of Opium—Golden Triangle Park in Chiang Saen will show the amazing three-thousand year history of opium.

This book shows the history of the last thirty years in northern Thailand. It is a story that should be known: People won, opium lost.

Bangkok
September 2001

Sandro Calvani
Representative
UNDCP Regional Centre for East Asia and the Pacific

INTRODUCTION

This book assesses how Thailand reduced opium production and use. Following crop replacement and integrated highland development projects in the 1970s and early 1980s, the government began eradicating poppies in 1984. Although cultivation declined far below the local consumption level by 1986, alternative development initiatives had to deal with new problems and correct shortcomings in the earlier efforts.

Many problems were encountered. Since so little was known about the hills, the ecological systems, and the people, when opium replacement started, mistakes occurred. These errors were compounded by barriers to working with people in the hills that were embedded within the Thai governmental system, such as regulations on land use and citizenship.

The interest generated in the hill people in Thailand by this development initiative as well as the need for more information on them encouraged dozens of anthropologists to study Thailand's highland groups. Many more studies were conducted on these peoples in the 1970s than in all the years preceding them. As these studies were conducted and the social scientists observed the difficulties encountered and the missteps made in trying to overcome them, negative assessments became commonplace.

Even harsher assessments came from such highly regarded members of the American Anthropological Association as Margaret Mead, who linked the Tribal Research Centre with a supposed (and unfounded) plot to eradicate the hill people.[1] Anthropologists entering the hills in the early 1970s were told to "stay away" from the Centre. Such warnings implied that the development projects be avoided as well.

These warnings imbued me with an implicit distrust of highland development work in northern Thailand. This influenced my own work on the highlands of northern Thailand which began with visits to hill villages in 1971 and has continued until the present.

Perhaps because I was a historian (tribal people were not commonly seen as having any history one could study), I was not warned to avoid the Tribal Research Centre when I entered the field in 1976. In any case, I had already been to the Centre and had talked to staff members in 1972 without becoming convinced that it was a dangerous organization. I had visited developers in the field and in their homes from that time on and seemed no worse the wear for it. So it did not seem unwarranted that the Tribal Research Centre should be my sponsor with the National Research Council for my

1. Probably the confusion began over a planned Tribal Data Centre begun in July 1969 and an organizational meeting held in January 1970 attended by representatives of forty-three agencies from the Advanced Research Projects Agency/Military Research Development Centre to the Catholic Mission in Chiang Mai. The former was supported by the CIA; this connection most likely was the cause of the suspicions by the anthropologists that escalated into a belief that in a mainframe computer kept in a basement the annihilation of the hill people would be plotted. Nothing so sinister was planned by the Thai side which wished to obtain basic socioeconomic data on these peoples. Plans for the meeting and the project make no mention of a basement or any kind of a computer.

doctoral dissertation work.[2] Still, though I had doubts about these projects that could be seen as trying to strip away the hill people's culture and fit them into the lowland Thai way of life. Having graduated from a California university in 1968 and thus belonging to a generation of student protesters, I viewed the links between the projects and the Vietnam War effort, at least in the early years, with suspicion.

Later when I returned to Thailand in 1980 with a doctorate, I found it ironic to be working for quite a few of the projects themselves. Beginning that year assisting in the baseline survey of the Mae Chaem Integrated Watershed Development Project, I eventually worked for half a dozen projects as a consultant, surveyor, translator, bean counter, and assessment team member. Although I never actually could find enough dirt on the projects to savage them in my reports (which in fact were generally positive), I could not shake the suspicions I had that the projects were intrinsically flawed.

So it was until July 2000 when Dr. Sanong Chinnanon of the UNDCP Regional Centre in Bangkok telephoned me to ask if I could write a report on how Thailand had reduced opium production. I thought he was joking. It seemed inconceivable that anyone would expect such a document to be produced. When at last I realized he was serious, it occurred that evaluating this highland development and opium eradication process would be intellectually challenging and probably of some practical importance. No one had yet comprehensively reviewed the work in the hills. Although UN and bilateral projects are subject to a continual process of

2. Organizations, such as the History Department of Chiang Mai University, that might logically have been willing to sponsor thesis research into the (mainly nineteenth-century) history of Tai-Karen relations declined the opportunity.

monitoring and evaluation, these assessments had not been linked to non-project work and other activities including road building, tourism, highland education, or the migration of hill people into the cities. The results of the report I would be writing would also be relevant to a whole range of projects in mainland Southeast Asia conceived in the image of project guidelines established in Thailand (albeit in countries with different highland policies from Thailand).[3]

During the writing of this project, I found others, even within UNDCP, that shared my suspicions. A regional project manager and country representative asked me how (in the world) I was going to write something acceptable to UNDCP headquarters in Vienna when "we all know" the problems of the Thai experience.

Once I began the work and studied the history of this process, I began to see the Thai experience in a new light. Although I cannot deny that I was almost incongruously disappointed that I would be obliged to render a positive verdict of the thirty year historical process, when I tried out my thesis on my fellow doubters, they were startled, responding, "Oh, well, that makes sense!"

A good starting point for this assessment is the estimate made by His Majesty King Bhumibol Adulyadej that replac-

---

3. One major difference is that in the countries neighboring Thailand, the hill people are citizens of that country. This was made apparent to me in 1995. On my first mission as the project manager of the UNDP Indochina Subregional Highland People's Programme, I went to Hanoi and met Vice Minister Phan Thanh Xuan, who was also vice chairman of the Committee for Ethnic Minorities and Mountainous Areas. When I told this formidable individual that Thailand had projects that Vietnamese officials might profit from visiting, he interjected, saying that "Thailand has [mistakenly] confused ethnicity with nationality," thus excluding tens of thousands of non-Thai residents from being Thai citizens.

ing opium would take thirty years. In the three decades since highland development began, the alternative development process evolved into a broad balanced approach comprising demand reduction, participatory community development, and law enforcement. Expanding beyond the UN, bilateral, and royal projects that pioneered the highland work, hill area activities are now integrated within the framework of the new ("People's") constitution of 1998 that grants considerable autonomy to *tambon* (village cluster) administrations and in which many NGOs work, too. Had such a unified and comprehensive approach existed when poppy eradication began, it is unlikely heroin use would have spread so quickly as it did in the hills and certainly the entire process would have gone faster. The participatory model that emerged, one which strongly influenced the concept of alternative development as adopted by the United Nations General Assembly, is one clear success of the Thai experience.

In writing this report, I wish to thank the UNDCP Regional Centre for East Asia and the Pacific, and UNDCP Headquarters in Vienna for their support. Thanks to the staff at the Regional Centre including its representative, Dr. Sandro Calvani, as well as Dr. Sanong Chinnanon, Mr. Bengt Juhlin, Mr. Wayne Bazant, Mr. Peter Lunding, Ms. Kaija Korpi, Ms. Lise Bendiksen, and Khun Thevee Kasemsuvan for all their assistance. Thanks too for help I received from the UNDCP Lao PDR country office staff in Vientiane, including its representative, Dr. Halvor Kolshus, and Dr. Marc Morival, manager of the C75 subregional demand reduction project dealing with high risk groups. Thanks also to the editing assistance of Silkworm in Chiang Mai. I am grateful for the help from all those I interviewed in different agencies (listed in the references) while writing this report. Although I had hoped to meet more people than I did in the hills who recalled the opium replacement projects, I am beholden to the many hill people I have met and learned from since I saw my first field of poppies in Mae La Noi District of Mae Hong Son in 1971.

Working with several highland projects during the 1980s and early 1990s was as much of a learning experience for me as it was for the others. We learned that reducing opium cultivation while developing the hills with local participation is tedious and trying, while the goals seemed unattainable. But there were enough successes in the Thai experience to show it can be done, many experiences to show that (eventually) it basically was done, and many indicators of how it might better be done elsewhere.

It is hoped that lessons learned from the Thai experience be used in other countries with diverse minority populations. It is also hoped that the lessons learned from Thai successes can be applied in Laos and Myanmar where opium production continues.

THE HISTORY OF OPIUM CULTIVATION IN THE GOLDEN TRIANGLE

The cultivation of opium as a cash crop came to Thailand in the late nineteenth century in the aftermath of Britain's Opium War with China in 1839–1842. To overcome a trade deficit with China, Britain wanted to trade opium grown in British India with China. Although the Chinese in the trading port city of Guangdong (Canton) objected, the British enforced its will through gunboat diplomacy. By 1858, the British were shipping 4,518 tons of raw opium annually to China. The Chinese nevertheless had refused to legalize the trade even though it had paid a huge fine after the Opium War, ceded Hong Kong Island, and opened several other coastal ports for trade with the British. When the British won the Second Opium War in 1858, the Chinese agreed to legalize opium (McCoy 1991, p. 82).

Local authorities in the south of China, where the opium poppy was already cultivated and used mainly for its medical properties, encouraged growing the poppy. By 1885, China was growing twice as much opium as it was importing and at the turn of the century, Chinese growers produced about 50,000 tons of raw opium per year. Half of this was grown in the uplands of Yunnan and Sichuan while most of the rest came from nearby provinces (Owen 1934, pp. 266–267; McCoy 1991, pp. 87–89).

The growers were mainly upland minority groups known to the Chinese as the Miao (sometimes spelled Meo) and Yao.[1] These terms represented general groupings of rural folk culturally different than and unfamiliar to the Han Chinese. In fact both Miao and Yao included many smaller and sometimes quite different ethnic units. Of those who moved to Thailand the best known Miao group is the Hmong and the best-known Yao group is the Mien.

Their movement south was primarily to flee fighting between warlords and bandits and rampant disorder in late nineteenth, early twentieth century southern China. As the minorities moved south, the cash-cropping of opium moved with them and an export trade from southern China to the big cities of Southeast Asia developed in the late 1800s. They generally settled at elevations over 1,000 meters where the opium poppy thrives in northern Thailand.[2] When opium growing became established in Thailand, growers and merchants in Thailand undercut the cost of supplying this market from China itself.

Among the Miao subgroups moving southwards, the Hmong were the most common. Over the years, the non-

1. There was diversity in these groups. Members of one Yao subgroup spoke a language in the Tai linguistic family. Such inconsistencies were not surprising. The Chinese were not ethnographers and they were unfamiliar with the languages spoken by the Miao and Yao whom they regarded as culturally inferior. Although the Hmong in Thailand prefer not to be called Miao, there are even more Miao in China who are not Hmong. As for the Mien in Thailand, they feel more comfortable being called Yao.

2. Thoughts of living at lower elevations were discouraged by the best areas in the lower hills being taken by Karen and Lua groups already in the area.

Hmong who did move south have assimilated into the Hmong. A similar phenomenon took place with the Mien; the major Yao group going south was the Mien. These people were joined in their movement by other groups such as Akha, Lahu, and Lisu who spoke Tibeto-Burman languages.

By World War II, opium cultivation in Thailand primarily supplied users in opium dens in the cities. Most users were Chinese, often laborers. In the hills, use was primarily medicinal but apparently there was also some recreational use. The total amount produced is unknown.

Following Mao Zedong's takeover of China in 1949, his government suppressed opium and its use throughout the country. Beginning in 1952, and using nationalistic and anti-American appeals in a campaign of mass propaganda and mobilization, the Chinese government first targeted drug trafficking in urban areas. Although the campaign was postponed in some minority areas in the south, China in the mid 1950s was essentially free of poppy cultivation and opium use (Zhou 1999, pp. 93–111).

To replace the opium lost to the world market, production in such Southeast Asian countries as Laos and Thailand increased. Poppy cultivation was possible in this region where opium production suited local conditions. The poppy grew well in the hills despite the poor tropical soils there. It required no advanced production technology nor did it need agricultural inputs such as chemical fertilizers or pesticides. The poppy had been grown in the region for several centuries making it resistant if not immune to local pests.

Furthermore, opium as a crop had advantages in terms of marketing and handling. No cold storage or sophisticated protection against spoilage was required. Aside from the banana leaves or handmade paper for the wrappers, opium required no special handling, did not need to be refrigerated, and required no specific types of packaging. Agents of the trafficking cartels provided agricultural inputs at the start of the growing season and appeared again in the village with money at harvest time. Soon after the agents bought the raw opium they "cooked" it rendering it into a state that preserved it for a long time. No other crop could equal these advantages in purely agricultural and commercial terms.

The main disadvantage opium production held was the unpredictability of the crop. A single rainfall during the harvest season before the latex can be scraped off, could ruin the crop. As a result, most cultivators customarily relied on a range of crops to reduce risk and insure their survival. Many villagers, for example, grew opium primarily to earn the cash to purchase enough rice for the year. Others raised a diversity of subsistence crops and a number of cash crops as well.

Fear of the increased production as a result of reduced cultivation in China may have been one reason why in 1955 the prime minister, Field Marshal Sarit Tanarat, issued a proclamation banning all production, sale, and use of opiates as of 1956. Other reasons given by the government for the ban were that opium cultivation was anachronistic and uncivilized. However, because of the heavy reliance the Thai government placed on revenues earned from the sale of opium, the Harmful Habit-Forming Drugs Act did not take full effect until 1959.

Even earlier, the Thai government had grown concerned over the hill people and border areas. Various agencies became involved with hill people starting in the 1950s.

In 1955, the government established the Border Patrol Police (as a special unit in the Royal Thai Police Department) to provide "control and public safety in the remote hills and frontier regions." Their work brought them into contact with the hill people for whom they sometimes built schools and distributed medical and agricultural equipment (Manndorff 1969, p. 8). Four years later, the government set up the Public Welfare Department that, among other responsibilities, became the lead agency working with hilltribes.

Government concern over forest resources and security issues grew in the 1950s. The Royal Forest Department with assistance from FAO conducted an aerial survey of forest resources in 1956–1957. The survey showed that well over half the forests in northern Thailand had been seriously degraded (Public Welfare Department 1964, pp. 12–13).

Although the hill people constituted only a small minority of all the forest dwellers in Thailand, they were culturally distinctive and engaged in shifting cultivation. Although various surveys have shown that if properly carried out, shifting cultivation (also called swiddening) preserves forest cover (see for example Zinke 1978, pp. 134–159) and even encourages certain types of wildlife, the RFD considered it anathema. Established in 1896 primarily to maximize the exploitation of teak through "scientific" forestry and to control the logging business, the RFD's purpose was to increase logging yields. The RFD considered shifting cultivation, which begins by burning down much of the forest cover to provide nutrients to raise crops, a waste of timber resources and a misuse of land that would be better used by growing tree crops. The high visibility of the hill people made it easy for the Royal Forest Department to single them out.

The cultural distinctiveness of the hill people had been worrying some officials for decades. They viewed the hill people as aliens in Thailand who did not belong to the "Thai Race." The spirit of Thai law at the time interpreted citizenship as something inherited from Thai parents. As early as 1921, local Thai officials wanted to evict a group of Hmong and Mien resisting efforts to draft them from Thailand. The officials wanted to burn their villages and force them across the border "because they were not Thai." Calmer voices prevailed and the government came to treat the hill people with benign neglect. This too changed as the Royal Forest Department gradually expanded its control to not just teak but all the country's forests and resources in them.

The government also worried about insurgencies in neighboring countries. In Laos, leftwing rebel groups had begun operating since about 1950 while rightwing groups joined the fray soon thereafter. Hmong were drawn into the conflict with different clans helping both sides at various times. Military and civilian leaders feared that the conflict would spread to Thailand among a group they perceived as aliens that had no "sense of belonging to any body or institution" (Public Welfare Department 1964, p. 14).

Thailand had no comprehensive highland development plan. Even as late as 1970, the Ministry of National Development barely mentioned the highlands, and the hill people not at all (1970).

Insofar as there was a plan, it was to solve the "problems of the hilltribes." In 1959, the Cabinet established the National Tribal Welfare Committee, chaired by the Minister of Interior, to oversee the hill people. However, due to a lack of funding and a clear program of activities, little was accomplished. The committee was reorganized several times through the 1970s but was unable to operate effectively.

In an attempt to instill loyalty in the hill people for Thailand and to control their activities, the government worked through the Public Welfare Department to establish a Self-Help Land Settlement Project for the Hilltribes in four border provinces: Tak, Chiang Mai, Chiang Rai, and Loei. Starting in 1960, Hmong and other groups were moved to lowland settlements (called *nikhom*) where they were to be taught agricultural methods appropriate for the lowlands as well as given a Thai education. However, because of insufficient inputs and resources, the *nikhom*, was not a viable alternative for the hill people.

The government asked international agencies for technical assistance and in studying the hilltribes. In 1965–1966, the Public Welfare Department surveyed socioeconomic conditions of the hill people. The next year, the United Nations Commission on Narcotic Drugs financed a survey team that investigated the social and economic needs of opium growing areas of northern Thailand in 1967.

The latter study estimated the area under opium cultivation to be approximately 18,500 hectares with a yield of 145 tons in the 1965–1966 season. To deal with this large level of production, the survey team advised that a large-scale effort would be required by the government in order to provide for the socioeconomic development of the hill people (United Nations Survey Team 1967, pp. 59–60). The government accepted the findings and the advice. Within the next few years, in cooperation with the United Nations, plans were drawn up for opium control measures in the hills.

At this time, opium was produced in Burma (now Myanmar), Laos, and Thailand. Opium production in Myanmar and Laos was even higher, estimated at approximately 800 and 200 tons respectively.[3]

Despite this high production, use in the region by growers was mainly for medicinal purposes. Most of the opium was exported by the minority groups to finance the insurgencies they were fighting against the national governments. Expatriate Chinese facilitated trafficking. Most was shipped out

---

3. Figures for these two countries are uncertain because most production was in insurgent areas where ground surveys could not be conducted.

through the excellent transportation infrastructure of Thailand to markets in North America and Europe.

A new market, among American soldiers fighting in Vietnam in the late 1960s worried the United States at a time when other substances such as marijuana and LSD were becoming increasingly popular in the West.[4]

Into this volatile situation came a name, the "Golden Triangle" which captured the imagination of the public and focussed attention on the area. Coined accidentally by U.S. Assistant Secretary of State (and later Ambassador) Marshall Green at a press conference on 12 July 1971, the term has taken on a life of its own. At a time just three days prior to President Nixon announcing he would visit China in February 1972, Green's calling the region a triangle (Burma, Laos, Thailand) implicitly recognized the absence of opium in China ("The Wonderland," 1971, p. 37). This term would come to evoke the lawless allure of opium and its trade. Within a few years, the Golden Triangle came to symbolize all of Southeast Asia's opium-related problems.

Just a few weeks earlier, one of Nixon's top advisors had flown to Thailand. This was Egil (Bud) Krogh, a White House deputy for domestic affairs who had earlier worked in John Erlichman's law office. He and others in the White House were under heavy pressure to bring a halt to the increased use of drugs, particularly heroin, in the United States.

A major American initiative was underway to interdict drugs at the source in such countries as Burma and Turkey, as well as Thailand. The United States was establishing a new means

---

4. Similar concerns at this time led in 1971 to the establishment in Thailand of an office of the United Nations Fund for Drug Abuse Control (UNFDAC) which combined the existing UN agencies in the regions dealing with narcotic drugs.

for countering drug use. Nixon had just set up the Special Action Office for Drug Abuse Prevention under psychiatrist Jerome Jaffe which was charged with demand reduction. The Cabinet Committee for International Narcotics Control, which was chaired by Secretary of State William Rogers, sought to interdict the flow of drugs into the United States (Krogh online interview).

When Krogh met Thai and UN officials at the American consulate in Chiang Mai, he delivered a message from the White House saying that the U.S. would support a crop substitution program that would stop the opium at its source. Present at the meeting were Col. Chavalit Yodmani from the Bureau of Narcotic Drugs and Mom Chao (Prince) Bhisatej Rajani representing the Royal Project, both of whom would play major roles in Thailand's drug control program for the next thirty years (Mann, personal communication, 2000).

Lisu harvesting poppy.

THE OPIUM TRADE

Poppy was grown for centuries by the family, mainly as a medicinal item. Only occasionally, when there was a surplus, did the hill people sell their opium. Trade in the substance was limited, attracting little attention from leaders of the major lowland kingdoms. Starting in the early nineteenth century, though, there is evidence that Yunnanese Muslim traders (known in northern Thailand as Haw) were bringing small quantities of opium from Yunnan for sale in Chiang Mai and other northern cities. Some opium also was imported by Arab and Chinese merchants to the coastal cities of Thailand including the capital of Ayutthaya. Although there is little information on this trade prior to 1800, there is no indication that opium was ever a major trade item in the past.

This changed following the Opium Wars in China. The decline of the Ching (Manchu) Dynasty in the nineteenth century gave rise to rebellion and general unrest in China's southern provinces such as Yunnan and Guangxi. As the Miao, Yao, and others moved south out of China into the kingdoms of Mainland Southeast Asia, they encountered Burmese, Thai, Lao, and other lowland groups.

Besides different Tai groups in the lowlands of Thailand, there were upland groups such as Lua and Karen who had lived in the region for centuries. To avoid conflict with them as well as to find an area where the opium poppy could provide ample yields, the Hmong and Mien found it convenient to settle at higher elevations.

Opium cultivation became legal in Thailand after 1855.[1] However, restrictions existed aimed at preventing its free cultivation. After initially allowing "tax farmers" to control the sale, the Royal Opium Monopoly was established at about the turn of the century to control opium production and sale.[2] By this, the government showed its desire to profit from the sale of opium in order to finance many government activities. The monopoly sanctioned certain growers to produce legal opium and then sell it to the government at controlled, generally low prices. By the 1920s, the artificially high prices charged opium users in the government dens made opium the country's largest revenue earner.

The Royal Opium Monopoly only bought from officially approved farmers. The monopoly paid the official rate and

1. This was the result of aggressive negotiating by the British diplomat John Bowring in the mid nineteenth century with the militarily weaker Thai government

2. Tax farmers bid for he right to sell opium (and other substances such as liquor, or other activities such as gambling). An agreement was made on how much each farmer would pay the government. Any income beyond that was profit for the tax farmer.

Government leaders, including the director of the Royal Opium Department, Prince Sithiporn Kridakara, wanted to stop opium cultivation. However, they recognized that doing so required armed intervention in Thailand and the cooperation of the British in Burma. The British Consul in Chiang Mai, W. A. R. Wood, advised the Thai that the British found it "undesirable and impossible" to comply within a limited time owing to the "great and unrenumerative expenditures" that would be required. The prince resigned, established an experimental farm in southern Thailand, and opium production continued.

sold it in the registered opium dens. However, the high mark-up charged in these dens encouraged illicit cultivation. Many den operators were willing to purchase non-official opium at a cheap price which they could then sell at the official price and make a large profit.

This profit came at a price. Growers of illegal opium moved into remote areas where they could sell their unsanctioned opium for more than the government buying price directly to den operators who could purchase the substance at less than the government selling price. This covert cultivation and smuggling created in this way criminalized opium decades before it was declared illegal.

This smuggling network was connected to the trade in British Burma. Since the Hague Opium Convention of 1912, the British had begun to restrict the use, trade, and cultivation of opium in Burma. Initially controls were implemented in the Burma Delta and the big cities of the country such as Yangon and Mandalay where there had been little use before the British era. British colonial officials deliberately left the Shan States,[3] site of many of the country's most lucrative production areas, beyond the area of controls. Besides helping fund British colonial activities, this arrangement facilitated cross-border smuggling, in particular, in the area of Kyaington, (Kengtung)[4] close to the Thai border.

The smuggling was overseen mainly by Chinese traders on both sides of the border. Although the Muslim Haw had

---

3. Now referred to collectively by the government as Shan State.

4. This place is referred to in many ways, almost all variations of Jengtung, which is how the local people, who call themselves Tai Khun, refer to the place. Contending that they are Tai and more closely related to the people of northern Thailand than the Western Shan, most city folk say it was the British who (mistakenly) started calling them Shan.

traded some opium in northern Thailand for well over a century, more populous groups of Chinese moved into Chiang Mai and other northern Thai cities in about 1900. Many were descendants of migrant laborers from southern Chinese provinces such as Guangdong and Fujian who had moved to work in and around Bangkok from the mid nineteenth century on. As they began to save money, many opened a wide range of businesses including tax farming and, later, managing opium dens. Some entrepreneurs established operations in the provinces.

In a process that has not been fully documented, these Chinese groups established links with the Haw and other traders from China. In this way, the smuggled opium both from within Thailand as well as from neighboring countries such as British Burma and China, came to be traded. By the start of World War II, the establishment of the Royal Opium Monopoly and its pricing system had resulted in a smuggling network that involved several neighboring countries. In remote areas, off the main roads, small villages near the border assumed considerable strategic importance. Wawi, in an old tea-growing area southwest of Chiang Rai, and other villages on Doi Tung and Doi Mae Salong mountains east and north of Chiang Rai, were some locations where Yunnanese Chinese settled, making them major marketing centers. Pha Mi, an Akha border village located just north of Doi Tung on a bluff overlooking the only access route in a narrow valley below grew into a popular trafficking route.

Major growing areas were scattered across the higher hills of northern Thailand.[5] In Chiang Rai, the slopes of Doi Chang,

5. No records exist detailing where opium was grown prior to about 1960 when the first government surveys were conducted. Information here is based on anthropological reports, interviews with hill people, government records of current cultivation, and other documents.

Mae Suai district, was a major growing area for Lisu and Akha. The Yao living in Phayao and Nan provinces near the Lao border cultivated large tracts. Hmong, who constituted the largest group, cultivated poppy in western Chiang Mai province, with such major growing centers as Mae Tho (Hot district), Mae Sa Mai (Mae Rim district), and on the western and eastern boundaries of Mae Chaem district, including Ban Phui in the south. A UN document refers to Mae Chaem as the "principal area of opium production in Thailand" (HAMP 1979). In Chiang Rai province, the eastern Lao border area of Wiang Kaen, opposite Laos, was another growing center populated by Hmong.

During World War II, the smuggling network was elaborated. The Thai government in 1942, realizing it could not resist the Japanese, decided to cooperate with the invaders. Partly in compensation, the Japanese gave Thailand parts of Cambodia and Burma that the Thais felt had been stolen from them by the French and British imperialism decades earlier. One was the Saharat Thai Doem (the Former Thai Confederation) province, including Kyaington, which was later occupied by the Northern Thai Army. Present in this army were future Thai prime ministers, such as Sarit Tanarat, KMT agents, and representatives of the U.S. Office of Strategic Services (later the CIA). During the war years, links in the network that facilitated exporting opium from southern China, the eastern part of British Burma, particularly beyond the Salween (Thanlwin) River, and upper Laos through Thailand were established. They would persist long after Saharat Thai Doem had been returned to British Burma in 1946.

Incised poppy capsule.

Poppy capsule.

16

OPIUM PRODUCTION AND CONSUMPTION

Traditionally, hill people ate raw opium, sometimes mixing it with substances such as garlic (Beno interview 2000). Opium was the most popular remedy for maladies such as pain, cough, dysentery, and the symptoms of malaria. The substance constituted the hill people's most effective medicine before the late twentieth century when modern health care reached the hills.

The hill people found that opium poppy was easy to cultivate in Thailand. All opium comes from the single species, *Papaver somniferum*, which belongs to the Papaveraceae family. Various cultivars from this species were identified by the growers that grow well in the north of the country. The opium poppy can be grown in either clay or sandy soils and does best in light and well pulverized sandy loams. The poppy can also be grown on level or sloping fields.

The opium crop is sown by broadcasting the seed in either September or October. Following periodic weeding and thinning, the plant is ready for harvest when it attains a height of about 100 centimeters in December or January. Ten days after the petals fall off, the growers incise the epicarp of the seed capsules to a depth of 1–2 millimeters with a curved metal tool. The depth of the slit is critical to the process because too deep a cut can cause the latex to drip onto the ground and too shallow a cut will cause the latex to harden within the capsule. Properly slit seedpods exude a milky latex that turns into a gumlike brown mass. The scraping can be repeated one or two more times until no more latex comes out. Because the seeds ripen unevenly, the harvest generally takes one to two weeks. Seed from high yielding plants are kept to sow the following year's crop.

Once harvested, the opium latex is rolled into balls that are wrapped in mulberry paper or banana leaves. This is what is usually called raw opium. Within approximately one month raw opium will lose about 15 percent of its weight because of evaporation. This affects the price and estimates of yield, subjects that will be discussed below.

Although opium was eaten when taking it as a medicine, some Hmong began to smoke it recreationally, a practice that in fact was influenced by the habit of smoking tobacco that came from the Americas.[1] Perhaps the most detailed description of smoking opium was written by an American physician, Joseph Westermeyer, regarding Hmong users. He wrote that small balls of opium, equal in size to a single pipeful, are prepared.

> Regular opium smokers usually had a small glass kerosene lamp, although older Hmong said that a lamp of pig fat was decidedly superior. Each ball of opium is placed on a small iron skewer and heated over the flame. As it begins to bubble and fume, it is deftly placed in the small aperture of the pipe. The smoker then places

---

1. Eating absorbs the active compound of opium more effectively. Smoking results in the loss of 80–90 percent being lost in the atmosphere. Eating is preferred because users find it more pleasurable as well as more convenient when they travel and do not wish to carry bulky smoking paraphernalia.

the pipe in his mouth as the flame is applied to the opium wad. With an opium lamp, this process is facilitated by reclining on one's side and holding the pipe so the aperture is horizontal to the ground . . . At the moment when the opium volatilizes from the heat, the smoker inhales deeply. Experienced users then contract their chest, abdominal and diaphragmatic muscles against a closed glottis so as to realize an optimal effect. This operation, called the Val Salva maneuver by physiologists, increases the intrapulmonary pressure and facilitates the rapid absorption of active opiate compounds across the pulmonary membranes directly into the blood stream. These compounds can be absorbed only from the pulmonary alveoli, not across the trachea and the bronchial tree (Westermeyer 1982, p. 57).

A single pipeful usually took twenty to thirty minutes to consume. Heavy users could spend hours a day smoking opium absorbed by its intoxicating aroma.[2] After enough pipes, even long-addicted users would become lethargic and doze off. Other ways of taking opium existed, such as taking it intranasally as a snuff. Opium in its volatilized form was also sometimes given as a medication by Hmong to infants to treat fever, diarrhea, or cough (Westermeyer 1982, p. 57).

Heroin did not become a popular illicit substance in Thai urban centers until Prime Minister Sarit Tanarat banned the cultivation, use, and trade of opium. He closed all the legal opium dens and tried to have the users detoxified and treated. However, the country lacked sufficient expertise in and facilities for drug treatment and rehabilitation. Many users

2. This is how users described it. Princess Vibhavadi remarked that the aroma was "like the inside of a porter's carrying bag—the smell was nauseous. All of us agreed on this. In the Royal Assistance Unit surely no one will become addicted" (Vibhavadi Rangsit 1997, p. 69).

continued to want to take opium. When it proved too difficult to obtain, users found heroin a satisfactory alternative.

Heroin is a refined opiate that retains morphine but not other alkaloids such as codeine that provided much of the substance's medical value. The refining process removes these alkaloids and about 90 percent of the volume of opium as well as its distinctive aroma, making it easier to smuggle. Even though the heroin that found its way into Bangkok first was only number 3 heroin (not as pure as number 4), its popularity grew through the 1960s and 1970s primarily in urban areas where opium was hard to obtain. There were few users in the hills mainly because opium was still readily available there.

Later, as shall be discussed below, when the opium poppy crop was reduced through development projects and eradication efforts by law enforcement agencies, heroin entered the hills. This occurred in the mid 1980s when Thailand became a net importer of opium and other changes occurred.

AN ECONOMIC OVERVIEW

MACRO-ECONOMIC CONDITIONS

Since World War II, Thailand has enjoyed sustained economic growth. Not only did Thailand survive the war years without experiencing major armed conflict, but international settlements in 1945 and 1946 enabled the country to join the United Nations in 1947 and experience the postwar years in stable economic condition. Not having suffered European colonization, having maintained its basic governmental system since the nineteenth century, and not having mobilized its army since 1824 also benefited the country's economy.

From 1951 until 1969, Thailand's gross national product rose from 35.2 to 112.4 billion baht, an average of 6.6 percent per year. After annual growth of 4.7 percent from 1951 until 1958, the rate of growth increased through the next decade to about 8 percent per annum (Ingram, 1971 pp. 221–223). Much of this growth came from agricultural exports. As world demand for agricultural products rose Thailand was able to exploit open land from 1950 until 1980 when 2.5 million new farms were created and total farmland doubled (Pasuk and Baker 1998, p. 23). The rate of growth represents a doubling of real income per capita about every eleven years. This growth

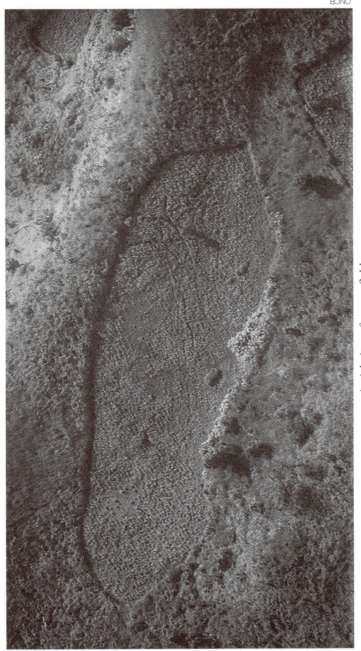

Aerial view of poppy field.

had a negative side as it contributed to a fall in the country's forest cover from 30 to 15 percent from 1960 to 1990.

The government facilitated this growth by continuing the rapid development of infrastructure that had started in the 1970s. New roads, dams, and irrigation projects were built to help open the new agricultural land. Besides encouraging investment (supported also by government incentives), new crops such as cassava, sugar cane, and pineapple became lucrative exports in the 1970s, growing at a cumulative rate of 12 percent per year. Food processing enterprises also grew at this time.

Two constraints in the 1970s that the country managed to overcome were increasingly high energy costs and the exhaustion of new agricultural land. Through discoveries of huge amounts of offshore natural gas and continued export growth, the country earned sufficient foreign exchange to manage its increasing debt. By the early 1980s, when little open land in the plains was unutilized, lowland agriculture intensified and many farmers moved into the foothills to cultivate crops. Government taxes on rice led to the development of non-rice crops with export potential (Pasuk and Baker 1997, p. 62).

The urban sector grew throughout. New banks were established and, after 1960, when protectionist tariffs were established, Thai firms manufacturing goods that replaced previously imported items flourished. Gradually, as these industrial concerns began producing goods for export, a number of increasingly large conglomerates dominated urban expansion.

These firms were generally dominated by first- or second-generation immigrants from southern China. Their emigration from southern China had been taking place since the mid nineteenth century. Many came from Swatow, Fujian, and Hainan where economic difficulties had grown amid internal rebellion in the mid nineteenth century. Leaving port cities such as Gwangzhou (Canton) and Xiamen (Amoy) to seek cash-earning opportunities elsewhere, from the gold fields of California to coolie labor in Bangkok and other cities in Southeast Asia, hundreds of thousands of migrants left southern China. Although many stayed in Thailand, others returned, out of which emerged a network linking the Overseas Chinese with those in China. Using these connections and links they had been setting up with Thai leaders from the early twentieth century on, these Chinese controlled the conglomerates that were pushing urban growth.

Thai citizenship laws and the preponderance of male migrants resulted in many Chinese settlers marrying Thai women. The Sino-Thai families and clans that resulted grew in power through the twentieth century, sometimes rose to great economic and even political power. By the 1960s, most of the country's major commercial banks and principal trading houses were run by these families. Rags to riches stories abound. To mention just two: a family in the pawn shop business expanded into real estate, establishing the Land and House real estate company capitalized at 62 billion baht in 1995 and a family known for selling silk grew to be the country's major telecommunication concern run by Thailand's richest man, and now prime minister, Thaksin Shinawatra (Pasuk and Baker 1998, pp. 48–49).

In the 1980s, the continued strength of the baht which had been pegged to the dollar, caused the cost of Thailand's agricultural exports to grow unattractively high. In response to this and other changes, the government devalued the baht twice and began to promote industrial growth that would allow the expansion of manufactured exports. In 1988, two years after Vietnam announced its Doi Moi (liberalization) policy, Thailand's general Chatichai called for *sanam rop* (battlefields) to become *sanam kankha* (marketplaces) and the country sought to dominate development in Mainland Southeast Asia.

Thailand's economy declined suddenly in 1997. The baht lost half its value in six months, falling from 25 to 50 to the U.S. dollar before recovering to 40 and then declining slowly to about 45. Although the rate of economic growth slowed, Thailand's economy and its infrastructure as well as human resource base remain the most vibrant in the lower Mekong subregion, attracting millions of legal and illegal migrants from many nearby countries.

MICRO-ECONOMIC CONDITIONS

Of all the people involved in opium producing, the growers profit the least. As opium moves out of the poppy fields, its price increases geometrically. Even the income made by the so-called "opium warlords" such as Khun Sa is slight compared with that made by the syndicates shipping what has now been refined into heroin to North America or Europe. Opiates were so lucrative they overrode politics. A Thammasat University student leaving Bangkok after the 6 October 1976 uprising, went to join insurgent troops near Doi Yao (future site of the Thai/UN Doi Yao/Pha Mon Highland Development Project) and found Communists growing opium to raise money (Chanthana 1993, p. 13).

Among the opium-growing groups in northern Thailand, the largest, most intensive cultivators were the Hmong. Although the Australian anthropologist, William Geddes, a prominent early student of Thailand's highland populations and a member of early UN opium surveys, viewed opium as the "mainstay" of the Hmong economy (1976, p. 201), he overstated the poppy's importance for them. Although patterns varied, most Hmong grew corn and rice in the rainy season months from about May until November and opium in the cold season from October until January. Sometimes they grew fruit trees, one type of which was a peach used for pickling, often earning them a considerable income. The Hmong raised livestock, hunted and gathered, manufactured handicraft, and engaged in cottage industry. A common opium growing pattern observed by Klein, another anthropologist, was that in years when opium production declined among the Lisu she studied, they produced more rice and vice versa (1990, p. 164).

In the case of the Hmong village of Khun Wang in Chiang Mai province, almost 120 hectares were used for growing the main crops of rice, opium, and corn. Less than 5 hectares were used for vegetables, fruit trees, and other crops such as tobacco and castor bean. Over three times as many days were spent working on the main crops than all the others together (Lee 1981, p. 99).

Livestock was important to the Hmong and the other tribes because through the 1970s very few roads reached into the hills and those that did were not paved and there were virtually no hill villages with a supply of electricity. The Hmong used ponies for transportation, buffalo and cattle for plowing and other such labor intensive tasks. Pigs, chickens, and sometimes goats were raised for food.

From the forest, the Hmong collected grass and other produce such as banana shoots to feed their beasts of burden. The villagers collected wood for fuel cooking fires that also provided warmth in winter. Fruits, tubers, and honey were also gathered as well as items for house building such as housing thatch and timber. The Hmong also foraged for pharmaceutical herbs, vines for rope making, and rattan for basketry. Without these forest products, the Hmong could not have survived.

By the 1970s, most big animals such as ox and tigers had been all killed near the opium growing areas. Hunting in Khun Wang and elsewhere was for smaller game such as barking deer, wild boar, porcupines, and jungle fowl. By the late 1980s most smaller game was exterminated and hunting grew less lucrative.

Growers raised opium by shifting cultivation, also known as swiddening.[1] Living on poor tropical soils, they burned the vegetation in order that their crops could thrive on the nutrients in the ash. After from one to three years, these nutrients were exhausted and new fields had to be cleared.

Two basic systems existed: pioneer swiddening and rotational swiddening. Pioneer swiddeners used a field once and then moved on to "pioneer" new areas with no idea of returning to the original place. Rotational swiddeners lived in one place and farmed fields near the village in rotation. After perhaps seven to ten years, soil fertility in the field returned and it could be cultivated again.

As practiced in the northern Thai hills, the practitioners of pioneer swiddening were mostly the migrants from Yunnan who raised opium. The groups such as Hmong, Mien, Akha, Lahu, and Lisu lacked attachment to local places and people in northern Thailand, aiming primarily to make a living in what seemed like an endless wilderness. Often, those who engaged in rotational swiddening, generally Karen and Lua

---

1. Swidden is related to *swidder*, and a variation of swither, derived from the Old Norse term, *svibre*, "to burn" (Oxford English Dictionary 1971 2: p. 343). The term was applied by the Swedish anthropologist, Izikowitz, to shifting cultivation for which no single one-word term existed that could be used as a noun or a verb.

peoples, had lived in the area and cultivated the same fields rotationally for centuries (Renard 2001).

There was sufficient land for both these farming systems to be employed until the 1960s. Opium cultivation could still be carried out throughout the northern hills at this time. Although population growth in the hills and the movement of lowland farmers out of the valleys, themselves becoming filled due to the expansion of agricultural fields, had begun putting pressure on land use in the uplands, there was still ample space for poppy fields in the 1970s.

Two other factors encouraged opium production in the mid twentieth century. First, the Royal Forest Department had begun reforesting rice fields in the hills, generally the fallow fields of rotational swiddeners. When growers found their swiddening cycle so restricted that there was not enough time for the forest to regenerate, they started growing more opium to earn cash to buy rice. Second, because most growers were not Thai citizens and lived in the forest, they were unable legally to own the land that could have served as collateral when they needed to borrow money. When these people needed a loan, they had to borrow from merchants in the area who either charged high interest or demanded payment in opium. The latter was easier for the hill people to obtain.

Yet it was also significant, and coincidental, that when opium cultivation in Thailand was reaching quite likely the highest it ever had been, farmers found themselves more open to alternative income sources in the hills. According to a Lisu elder, by the mid 1960s, the government had warned the hilltribes on Doi Chang to abandon opium growing. Although little poppy destruction was carried out for another two decades, the growers were becoming apprehensive about the illegality of the crop and possible sanctions the government might take against them.

Opium poppy yields varied by ethnic group. Whereas the Lisu in Doi Chang and the Hmong of Mae Tho and Khun Wang in Chiang Mai earned yields of 1.5–5 kilograms of opium per rai, the Yao of Pulangka earned almost twice that (Miles 1974, p. 230). Nevertheless, the mixed economy of the Hmong was also found among the Yao, Lisu, and other groups. Lee, the Hmong anthropologist, compiled more complete data than other researchers at the time on Hmong economic activities (Lee 1981, p. 162). Data on their income from opium as well as from other sources is shown below. In the 1970s, many Hmong (and other groups) made their own clothes, though some bought clothes from their neighbors. Although some hill groups such as Karens grew cotton, the Hmong used hemp for their cloth. Some older people could still make their own jewelry and ornaments, but most purchased them from the Mien (Yao). Other village industries included blacksmithing and woodworking. As time passed, more and more of their utensils, such as sickles, axes, and plastic containers, were bought from lowland markets. Conversely, an increasing number of Hmong handicrafts were sold to lowlanders, tourists, and others.

Below are figures for Hmong income in the village of Khun Wang. The data were collected by Lee who selected Khun Wang as his research site because it was one of the first UN project's key villages. Although it can be assumed he used his ethnic ties with the villagers well and obtained accurate data, the figures do not represent an "undeveloped" village. It should be noted that in addition to the cash income detailed below, there were also various items collected from the forest for home consumption. The actual income of the Hmong thus was greater than the actual cash figures noted in table 1.

Khun Wang is located on the eastern flank of Doi Inthanon, Thailand highest mountain and located southwest of Chiang

Fish pond, rice paddy, and coffee plantings, Khun Wang

Table 1
ANNUAL HOUSEHOLD INCOME,
HMONG OPIUM GROWERS IN CHIANG MAI PROVINCE

SOURCES VALUED IN BAHT OBTAINED IN CASH/OPIUM	1976		1977	
	CASH	OPIUM*	CASH	OPIUM*
Sale of opium crop	422,120	–	189,630	–
Sale of peaches	24,330	–	3,828	–
Sale of domestic animals	24,255	10	40,720	200
Sale of farm products	1,750	–	1,880	–
Interest from loans/bank	7,670	–	2,700	–
Wage labor	1,175	1,050	3,925	860
Sale of game and crafts	3,600	–	1,770	80
Family business	4,630	–	3,920	–
Salaries	3,600	–	12,000	–
Performing rituals	220	400	555	1,100
TOTAL IN BAHT	490,777	1,460	260,928	2,150

(Lee 1981, p. 162)

Notes: US$ = 20 baht; opium price averaged 1,562.5 baht per kilogram in 1976 and 937.5 baht per kilogram in 1977.
*Data in this column is the cash value of the opium obtained from each source.

Mai. Although there was flatland around the village settlement area, slopes in the village ranged from 16–85 degrees making it difficult to find suitable rice-growing areas. Khun Wang was far from self-sufficient in rice. In 1977, Lee found that on 15.44 hectares of swiddened and terraced rice fields, about 44,000 kilograms of rice was produced, enough for only 58 percent of the village's needs. Ample cultivation of opium was needed to provide the cash to pay for the remainder of the village's rice needs (Lee 1981 pp. 157–159). Although Khun Wang's economy was dominated by income from the sale of opium poppy, the data does show a variety of income sources. Previously the price of peaches had been high but the market for them collapsed in about 1976.

Lee asks whether these figures support the common belief that an opium producer makes a better living than an ordinary Thai. The table above notes that the gross annual household income was 16,407.6 baht in 1976 and 8,769.3 baht in 1977. The average monthly household income for all villagers in Thailand's seventeen northern provinces was 1,318 baht for 1975–1976 (NSO Report 1976, p. 38). Although the highlanders have a lower income, the hill people could utilize much of the materials they collected from the forest so that in fact their standard of living was probably somewhat better than the average poor urban dweller. In years with high yields, the opium growers earned more cash income than most rural Thais. Nonetheless, they were far from wealthy, had little disposable income, and hoped they could improve their standard of living.

THE ECONOMICS OF OPIUM
PRODUCTION

Estimating opium production has always been difficult. In the early 1900s, when the Royal Opium Monopoly of Thailand controlled opium production, it only allowed certain growers to cultivate the poppy. This was meant to ensure that the monopoly controlled the supply, distribution, and retail price of opium, by which the government intended to raise a large amount of revenue. In doing this, the government sold its opium at almost twice the market price of opium in British Burma, opening the way for rampant smuggling. This was only encouraged by the fact that Thai opium reputedly tasted less appealing than certain types from British Burma (Supaporn 1980, pp. 136–139).

Problems associated with estimating opium production are manifold. Difficulties are evident in the earliest figures on the subject in Thailand. For 1917, records of the Office of the Financial Advisor to the Thai government noted that opium was produced in three provinces as shown in table 2 (Supaporn 1980, p. 138).

These officially sanctioned fields of course were not the only opium fields in Thailand. Besides the imported opium, some was also illegally cultivated. The growers generally sold this to owners of unlicensed opium dens as well as the official ones.

Table 2
PROBLEMATIC STATISTICS ON OPIUM PRODUCTION IN
NORTHERN THAILAND (1917)

AREA	AREA CULTIVATED (RAI)	AMOUNT OF RAW OPIUM	METRIC WEIGHT
Chiang Rai	1,000	100,000 tamlung[1]	6,000 kilograms
Nan	750	75,000 tamlung	4,500 kilograms
Den Chai	100	10,000 tamlung	600 kilograms
Total	1,850	185,000 tamlung	11,100 kilograms

The managers of the latter would thus sell the opium at less than the government rate. When they could pass off the illegal opium as legal, they could increase their income significantly.

This desire of the government to raise revenue from opium thus contributed to establishing a criminal network clandestinely transporting the substance throughout the country. This network has survived to the present and has facilitated the shipment of other illegal substances and items.

For all sites noted above the yield is given equally as 6 kilograms per rai (1,600 square meters, 0.16 hectare), which suggests that those calculating the yield had not made estimates in the field. Also, the high yield of 6 kilograms per rai is about six times more than Hmong yields and three times more than Yao yields in the 1960s and 1970s. Since it is unlikely the growers themselves made these high estimates, these figures may represent Bangkok officials trying to optimize tax revenues. These officials, who were well aware of both the smuggling and the likelihood that growers were cultivating poppies on more fields than those authorized, most

1. A tamlung is equal to 4 baht in weight, or 60 grams. In the old system of weights and measures of Southeast Asia, 100 tamlung equals 1 viss, a term still used in Myanmar.

likely made artificially enhanced calculations to obtain what they thought was the appropriate amount of revenue.

Similar problems persisted in the 1960s when the first serious effort to estimate opium production in Thailand was made by the Public Welfare Department (1962). Prior to this the government did not collect its own data on opium cultivation in any statistically useful way. Although not conducting field measurements, the 1962 survey team did visit poppy growing areas in Tak, Chiang Rai, and other provinces where they interviewed growers and inspected some fields, mainly Hmong and Lisu.

The Public Welfare Department team estimated that one person could cultivate one rai per year from which a yield of about 1 kilogram (or less) could be earned and that one family worked four rai on the average. In 1962, the price for one kilogram of raw opium in the hills was 800–900 baht. Accordingly, the hill people earned a total of 54,440,000 (then over US$2 million), or approximately $250 per hectare (Public Welfare Department 1962, pp. 62–65; United Nations Survey Team 1967).

A second survey was conducted in 1965–1966 that involved field inspections, a detailed evaluation of poppy yields, and aerial surveys. The results from this were that 145 tons of opium was produced in the country, a figure that stunned Thai leaders.

Two years after the establishment of ONCB in 1976, Thailand had begun conducting its own opium cultivation surveys. The increasingly sophisticated tools that ONCB used were challenged by ingenious farmers. Using techniques learned from the development projects, such as intercropping opium with other crops to conceal the poppy and growing during the off-season, ONCB faced increasing difficulties in finding the fields. By 1997, ONCB used ground surveys as

Table 3
OPIUM PRODUCTION IN THAILAND: 1961–1999 [a]

YEAR	AREA (ha.)	PRODUCTION (kg.)	KG/HA	PRICE baht/kg.	PRICE $US	GROWERS INCOME baht	GROWERS INCOME $US
1961/62[b]	12,112	64,000		850	43	54,440,000	2,722,000
1965/66	17,920	145,600	8.0	500	25	72,800,000	3,640,000
1980/81	6,026	48,565	8.1	1,500	71	72,487,500	3,451,785
1981/82	7,391	57,178	7.7	1,500[c]	71	85,767,000	4,084,143
1982/83	5,531	33,527	6.1	1,750[c]	76	58,672,250	2,550,967
1983/84	6,933	35,949	5.2	2,000[c]	87	71,898,000	3,126,000
1984/85[d]	8,290	33,560	4.0	2,500	109	86,685,000	3,768,913
1985/86	2,428	16,510	6.8	2,500	109	41,275,000	1,794,565
1986/87	592	3,848	6.5	2,750	120	10,582,000	460,087
1987/88	2,811	16,866	6.0	3,000	130	47,410,326	2,661,319
1988/89	2,982	29,820	10.0	3,500	152	174,881,000	7,603,522
1989/90	782	8,602	11.0	3,200	139	27,526,400	1,196,800
1990/91	355	5,680	16.0	3,400	136	19,312,000	772,480
1991/92	869	9,994	11.5	3,500	140	34,979,000	1,399,160
1992/93	999	14,381	14.4	7,500	300	107,857,500	4,314,300
1993/94	479	3,228	6.8	7,500	300	24,210,000	968,400
1994/95	169	7,113	13.25	8,000[e]	320	56,904,000	2,276,160
1995/96	368	12,581	12.5	10,000	400	125,810,000	5,032,400
1996/97	252	17,016	11.25	10,000	400	170,160,000	6,806,400
1997/98	770	16,974	11.25	20,000	400	339,480,000	6,789,600
1998/99	702	7,899	11.25	20,000	500	157,980,000	3,949,500
1999/2000	330	3,712	11.25	20,000	500	74,240,000	1,856,000

[a] Figures for 1961 and 1965 are from Public Welfare Department, 1962 and United Nations Survey Team, 1967. For 1980–1988, see ONCB's annual reports for Thailand; for subsequent years, see ONCB's Opium Cultivation and Eradication Reports. ·

[b] Figures are based on the reinterpretation of Public Welfare Department, 1962 by United Nations Survey Team.

[c] Estimated figure

[d] From 1984 on, when the government began a program to eradicate opium poppy, the area is calculated by subtracting the amount destroyed from the amount cultivated. In cases where the same plot was cultivated more than once, the area is calculated to include each time a plot is cultivated. See ONCB's Opium Cultivation and Eradication Report for 2000 for figures, methodology and other details. The yield is based on the amount of opium an average hectare produced before destruction efforts. It should be noted that in 1930, the government reported poppy eradication had been carried out in the north (Commission of Enquiry 1930 I, p. 87).

[e] Price represents average estimates calculated by ONCB.

Table 4
OPIUM PRODUCTION IN MYANMAR, 1964–1999

	AREA (ha.)	PRODUCTION (tons)	KG/HA	PRICE (kg.)	GROWERS INCOME
1964	30,000	300–400	1.97	$12.50	$4,375,000
1967	36,382	360	1.78	16.50	5,940,000
1977	70,000	500–800	1.78	–	approx: 10,000,000
1987–1988	–	1,000–1,500	1.78	–	"
1988–1989	–	about 1,500	1.78	–	"
1989–1990	–	about 1,500	1.78	–	"
1990–1991	–	about 1,500	1.78	–	"
1991–1992	–	about 1,500	1.78	–	"
1999–2000	–	about 800	–	–	–

From 1987 on, the size of the opium-producing area varies too widely to make useful estimates.

Sources: U.S. Department of State, 1992, p. 259; Myanmar CCDAC 1991; UN Survey Team 1992; United Nations 1967, p. 74; U.S. Congress 1978, pp. 6,10; Renard 1996, pp. 102–105; UNDCP Myanmar 2001.

Table 5
OPIUM PRODUCTION IN LAO PDR, 1966–1992

	AREA (ha.)	PRODUCTION (kg.)	KG/HA	PRICE (kg.)	GROWERS INCOME
1966–1967			4–6	$10–12	–
1971–1972			4–6	$14–15	–
1974–1975	6,465	38,790	6	$20–25	775,800
1991–1992	19,190	126,654	6	–	–
1999–2000				$40–400	–

Sources: Westermeyer 1981, pp. 42–44; Lao National Commission for Drug Control and Supervision 1993, vol. 1, pp. 18–20.

well as aerial surveys with the Royal Thai Police Aviation Division and the Royal Thai Army. LANDSAT and SPOT satellite imagery was also studied and analyzed by software processing systems (ONCB 1999, pp. 5–7).

Despite the obstacles, ONCB's surveillance has led to the destruction of at least half the crop every year since 1985.[2] The effectiveness of the surveillance and eradication work by ONCB apparently has resulted in a change in strategy by a cartel which seems to control the price of opium throughout northern Thailand and areas of Laos close to Thailand. According to ONCB analysts, from 1997 on the cartel began hiring farmers in Thailand to grow the poppy experimentally, under multiple conditions to learn how to maximize yield and avoid detection. This is confirmed by the price of opium being unusually high at the start of the growing season when, ONCB believes, the cartel is engaging the growers. There are anecdotal accounts that a kilogram of raw opium grown for hire so that the cartel can experiment runs as high as 100,000 baht per kilogram (about $2,380 at the current exchange rate of 42 baht to US$1.00. The devaluation of the baht from 25 baht/US$1.00 in 1997 to 42 has contributed to increased prices for opium in baht.

A dual price structure for opium in Laos seems to confirm the ONCB analysis. Opium from areas close to the Thai border such as Oudomxay commanded high prices, not far from what Thai farmers get. For reasons that are unclear, opium from Bolikamsay on the Vietnam border was quite

---

2. Opium production was already declining because of the crop replacement and highland development projects. Officials believed in 1984 that since viable alternative sources of income existed, a balanced approach combining eradication with the development initiatives would be more productive.

high: 3,611,000 kip/kg ($498).[3] More understandably, opium from Phongsaly in the far north near China was much cheaper: 309,000 kip/kg ($43). Because the 2000 UNDCP Lao opium survey had insufficient data for some provinces, it is impossible to estimate how much money reaches the farmer in individual provinces.

Some cultivators have crossed into Myanmar where surveillance is less prevalent. Myanmar remains by far the biggest producer in the region at about 1,500 tons followed by Laos, at about 126 tons. The relatively little that Vietnam produces is used domestically or just across the border in China where almost no opium poppy is grown.

Statistics for opium production in Myanmar are harder to calculate than in Thailand. In the 1960s and 1970s much opium was grown in insurgent-controlled areas making ground surveys impossible. Political factors may have also influenced estimates. Lack of information about local conditions precludes knowing how much income reaches the growers. Nonetheless, the preliminary figures in tables 3, 4, and 5 give some idea of the situation.

LESS OPIUM, MORE HEROIN

As the government extended its control over the hills, more pressure was put on opium growers. Opium cultivation declined although the reasons for reducing poppy growing differed radically. Based on the accounts of two social scientists familiar with conditions in the hills, the farmers in the following two locations indicate reasons why opium cultiva-

---

3. At the exchange rate of 7,250 kip to the U.S. dollar in the year 2000.

Poppy eradication.

tion declined, as well as some of the problems related to the reduction of poppy growing.

DOI CHANG VILLAGE, MAE SUAI DISTRICT, CHIANG RAI PROVINCE

In 1988 the reasons given by farmers for ceasing to grow opium in 1986/1987 was that as long as TG-HDP was there and they had a firm market for their cabbages and tomatoes they were willing to conform overtly to requests originating with the authorities (ONCB/Public Welfare Department). This included greatly reducing the size of, and scattering their poppy fields so they could not be found so easily. Where possible they relocated cultivation to areas that were not under such close surveillance. They also willingly participated in the incendiary public theater of throwing their opium smoking gear on to a large bonfire. Another incentive, especially for the Akha, was the opportunity to regularize their residential status in Thailand. Although some attention was given to commencing citizenship negotiations, the ID cards issued to coffee growers were of more immediate interest, more important in fact for their semiotic significance than anything else.

The 1989 season was particularly bad. When the crops were ready to harvest the road became virtually impassable, the price of tomatoes dropped to next to nothing, and the cabbages were so heavily treated with lethal sprays and smelled so bad that truckers from Bangkok refused to load them. Tomatoes and cabbages rotted in the fields. By this time the Thai-German Project had moved on to other activities and new areas so it did not have to face up to the price the community was paying for going along for adopting the introduced crops. In that season three men died of respiratory arrest most probably caused by spraying insecticides, and two young women committed suicide because it had become clear that their

41

families would never have enough money to assemble the bride price that was held at a relatively high level (McKinnon personal communication).[4]

PANG KHA VILLAGE, CHIANG KHAM DISTRICT, PHAYAO PROVINCE

By the time of Douglas Miles' research (1974) carried out in 1966–1967, most if not all of the opium fields of Pang Kha (Pulangka) were located away from the village, at a place called Ban Meo Mo, a Hmong village then entangled in the "Red Meo Revolt." The road, built in 1967 or 1968, greatly influenced the villagers' decision to stop growing opium because it exposed them to inspection. My guess is that opium growing became too costly or dangerous for people living near a road. In this time of insurgency, unless traders came to them, doing any kind of business on their own was risky. Even men who went courting were arrested on suspicion of being a Communist infiltrator. This is different from the Mae Chan area, where access to "Chinese" traders was greater. So, the presence of the CPT in the hills contributed to making opium farming too difficult because of all the official attention and the counter-insurgency warfare. The criminalization of the *chao khao* (hilltribes) may have been greatest in this area, including southern Chiang Rai and northern Nan, from the late 1960s and through the 1970s. The hills were also a free-fire zone from early 1968 on, for several years. All the Mien left the highlands for years (Jonsson, personal communication).

4. According to ONCB 2000, small pockets of poppy cultivation remain.

Once the decision to eradicate poppy was made by Thai authorities, prices increased substantially, from about 500 baht per kilogram of raw opium in 1981 to five times that in 1988, and more subsequently. The increased use in heroin was also caused by reported increases in production among autonomous groups near the Myanmar-Thai border. Simultaneously, the technology of refining heroin was reportedly transferred from the Yunnanese Chinese to the Hmong (Anek and Suwannarat 1994).

ONCB officials say that the first serious outbreak of heroin use was among Hmong in the old HAMP village of Mae Sa Mai, north of Chiang Mai. From here it spread to many villagers, Hmong and Karen in particular (Mann 1994). By 1994, heroin use had spread to over 150 villages affecting 5,000–6,000 people. As this occurred, more attention was devoted to all forms of rehabilitation and drug treatment.

A major question is whether reducing the opium supply below the domestic usage level in Thailand contributed to heroin use. In the twentieth century, a decline in opium use has occurred many times just prior to an increase in heroin use. Examples are the United States in the 1920s, and Australia as well as Bangkok in the 1950s. There possibly may not, however, be a cause and effect relationship between the two. The rapid growth of heroin use in other places, such as in Pakistan, during the 1980s may be attributable to other factors. Similarly, no decline in the use of heroin, the drug of use at the time, immediately preceded the rapid increase of amphetamine use in Thailand in the mid 1990s. The use of individual drugs can change free of links to other drug use. In Thailand, as shall be discussed below, the transition from opium to heroin use occurred at a time of considerable change.

What is clear, though, is that the opium replacement projects in operation at the time lacked a truly participatory nature and gave too little attention to drug demand reduction and prevention. Lacking the comprehensiveness of appropriate alternative development work, the activities in the 1980s were insufficient to impede the introduction of new narcotic drugs.

NATIONAL HIGHLAND DEVELOPMENT POLICIES

NATIONAL ECONOMIC AND SOCIAL DEVELOPMENT PLANNING

Thai national development policy is stated in the National Economic and Social Development Board's (NESDB) five-year economic and social development plans. The government began preparing such plans in 1961 when the per capita gross national product of Thailand, 1,600 baht, was less than several Sub-Saharan countries. Since then the per capita GNP has increased forty-seven times suggesting that these plans played a role in encouraging Thailand's subsequent economic growth.

By the end of the first three plans (1961 to 1976) which were designed to promote the free enterprise system, considerable economic growth had occurred. During the 1970s, the country's cooperation with the United States during the war in Cambodia, Laos, and Vietnam, major infrastructure development took place. Through the course of these events, an income gap developed and widened considerably during the Third Plan. The Fourth and Fifth Plans promoted industrialization, in particular through the Eastern Seaboard Development Program.

Concern over social issues arose during the Fifth Plan when the Rural Development Plan was introduced to solve problems of rural poverty that now extended beyond the income gap. The government perhaps took a cue from the king's interagency Development Study Centres, where agencies responsible for development were linked through working committees at different administrative levels. During the implementation of these plans, Thailand's economy grew rapidly, in 1989 reaching the exceptionally high level of 12 percent, making it one of the fastest growing in the world.

Concern for social issues continued during the Sixth Plan (1986–1991) when the development of "human quality" was promoted. People's participation was recognized, essentially for the first time, in the Sixth Plan. At this time, highland development was rethought in the formulation of the Rural Development Plan. Three main objectives were identified for hill area work:

- establish permanent settlements
- reduce areas under opium poppy cultivation
- conserve natural resources, in particular the watersheds

To accomplish these objectives, the following priorities were set:

- identify areas suitable for the introduction of administrative measures (such as legalizing villages)
- prepare an integrated master plan and establish cooperation among the principal government departments
- extend basic health services,
- improve infrastructure for development.

In the Seventh Plan, for 1992–1996, NESDB sought to convert rapid economic growth to sustainable growth with stability (UNDP 1992, pp. 18–19). This type of planning continued through the Eighth Plan that was drafted in cooperation with an NGO umbrella organization and finalized in 1996 as the People's Development Plan. This Plan stresses people's participation, the importance of civil society, and role of local governmental agencies such as the *tambon* council.

MASTER PLANS FOR THE HIGHLANDS

Even prior to the highland component in the Rural Development Plan devised under the Sixth Plan, the government had identified problems in the Thai hills. In the early 1960s, the government began to be concerned over a hilltribe "problem" and drew up a five-year plan for implementation in 1964–1969. The plan called for the Department of Public Welfare, the Border Patrol Police, and the Central National Security Command, to conduct crop replacement and other development activities. In an address at the dedication of the Tribal Research Centre in Chiang Mai in 1964, the director general of the Public Welfare Department identified main objectives for government work with the hilltribes (Aran 1976, pp. 25–26):

1) prevent forest and watershed destruction,
2) end opium cultivation,
3) arrange for socioeconomic development of the hilltribes, and
4) instill a feeling of loyalty to Thailand among the hilltribes.

The government could not implement the plan comprehensively or effectively. The lack of adequate funding, unfamiliarity of the government officials with hill areas impeded work. Although, as described below, funding for crop replacement work was obtained, there was no opportunity to carry out the work in a balanced fashion.

Only in the 1980s would the situation change so that a more integrated effort could be implemented. The government had by then grown determined to bring unity to the fragmented nature of highland development that would take place in the 1970s.

Influenced by incidents such as in the Mae Chaem Project where, in 1981, USAID refused to provide funding until the Royal Forest Department issued land use permits (see below, page 93) as called for in the project paper, the Cabinet reviewed highland issues. In December 1982, the Cabinet passed another resolution entitled "A Brief Account on Government Resolution Towards Problems of Hilltribe People and Opium Production," which confirmed the government's support of socioeconomic development of the hilltribes as the most effective way to eliminate poppy cultivation and opium addiction.

To create a unified approach to highland activities, the Cabinet identified agencies it saw as working in areas of concern for hill people. These agencies, which were to "lead" the work, included four "basic" ministries: the Ministry of Agriculture and Cooperatives, the Ministry of Education, the Ministry of Public Health, and the Ministry of the Interior, as well as the Bureau of the Budget, NESDB, and the National Security Council. The Ministry of Education later drew up a new curriculum for highland development including a nonformal education plan, and the Ministry of Public Health devised a health care delivery model for hill areas (NESDB 1988, pp. 49–50).

NESDB's First Master Plan for the Development of the Opium Poppy Cultivation Regions of Thailand in 1983 (ONCB 1983) proposed eight rural development projects comprising 37 percent of the estimated poppy growing regions in the country and over half of the areas not already covered by the then existing projects.[1] National and Provincial Hilltribe Committees were established that comprised representatives of the four "basic" ministries. Also set up were Provincial Hilltribe Welfare and Development Centers through which the Department of Public Welfare operated and to which hilltribe development projects reported (Francis et al. 1991, pp. 13–14).

Concerns that hill people threatened national security had existed since the late 1950s. As a part of the highland planning underway, the National Security Organization established the Committee to Facilitate the Solution to National Security Problems Relating to Hilltribes and the Cultivation of Narcotics Crops (COHAN). COHAN was established in 1987 with a deputy prime minister as chair. One COHAN duty was to facilitate coordination between provincial level organizations and to monitor development (COHAN 1990, p.8). COHAN arranged meetings of agencies working in the hills, including national and international NGOs as well as church groups to inform them of government policy.

Other concerns existed. Influenced by incidents regarding such issues as land-use permits in Mae Chaem, some government officials concluded that the First Master Plan gave too much authority to project donors and implementing agencies. In response, the government asked ONCB, with help from

---

1. Most of these proposed rural projects were implemented and are discussed below.

UNDCP, to draw up a Second Master Plan for Highland Development and Drug Abuse Control.

This master plan, completed in 1988, called for highland development to occur through Thai governmental organizations. Project activities were integrated into the national administrative structure. Instead of being project- or donor-driven as before where an Egil Krogh could influence national policy, activities under this master plan were to follow planning by provincial, district, and *tambon* planning units. This approach followed the National Rural Development Plan that was drawn up as a part of the Sixth Plan (Francis et al. 1991, p. 14) which was to establish permanent settlements.[2] As noted above, the main priorities were to "settle down" the hill people, reduce opium cultivation, and conserve the environment.

Under the Seventh Plan, yet another master plan was devised: the 1992–1996 Master Plan for the Development of Highland Populations, Environment and Control of Narcotic Crops. The most important innovation of this master plan was provisions for sustainable growth and people's participation. Emphasis was placed on permanent agriculture, improving the standard of living, distributing income more equitably, and developing human resources.

Several years of planning involving agencies and organizations representing much of Thai society led to the drafting and adoption of the "People's Constitution" in 1998. Drawing its authority directly from the people, the new constitu-

2. The idea that hill people must be settled down in the valleys is not new. Jesuit priests in the Spanish Philippines had brought "considerable numbers" of "mountaineers" into the valleys in the nineteenth century and earlier (Worcester 1913, p. 1160).

tion decentralized power, giving much authority to local organizations.

In this spirit, the Tambon Administration Organization Act was passed. With this act, almost all government agencies in the *tambon* (including schools and clinics) come under the *tambon's* administrative control. People's participation in this process will be active.

These administrative provisions extended into the hills, integrating almost all the highland villages directly into the national administrative system. This all but eliminates the need for future highland master plans.

PROBLEMATIC ISSUES

Despite efforts by the Thai government, it was impossible to create a comprehensive and integrated approach to dealing with the hill people. Two issues resisted efforts to find solutions for decades. At present, the issues of forest use and citizenship remain unresolved, although both may be solved soon by recent policy changes.

FOREST USE

The Royal Forest Department became more directly involved in hilltribe work when its watershed classification zone scheme was endorsed by a Cabinet resolution in 1985. Six major classes were established: 1A, 1B, 2, 3, 4, and 5. Class 1A watersheds are meant to be completely protected from all human use. Lower zones are progressively more open to use with Class 5 open to almost all agricultural practices.

The regulations by the Royal Forest Department did not solve all the problems of people in the hills. Disagreements occurred with other agencies, governmental and non-governmental, working with people in forests. Even after the almost total eradication of opium, many highland groups faced resettlement out of national parks and other reserves in areas they had sometimes inhabited for centuries. The amount of area declared as a national park has increased in recent years, intensifying the problem. Outright resettlement has not happened too often because of clauses in the regulations saying that hill people can only be resettled in areas comparable in quality to those abandoned. Since little such land remains, officials have not often resorted to resettlement.

Another issue is community forests. Various groups and agencies have been pushing for local people to have the right to use forests in and around their village. A community forestry bill has been drafted. Although making some progress through the Parliament, it is not yet law. The Community Forestry Division of the Royal Forest Department is in disagreement with other divisions of the RFD over how community forestry should be implemented (or if it should be at all). Vested interests and certain developers also have opposed community forestry because they see it as preventing them from exploiting various rich forested areas.

These regulations made highland development work more difficult, if not impossible.

CITIZENSHIP AND LOYALTY

Thai citizenship has been another complicating factor in replacing opium and developing the Thai hills. When Thailand first accepted the concept that it was a nation-state and that it had citizens (rather than subjects as before), the Thai government was eager to make all the minority groups indigenous to the region citizens. Government officials in Mae Hong Son in 1889 went so far as to force Red Karens to be tattooed with the sign of a white elephant on their arms to show they were Thai citizens (IO 1889).

During the reign of King Chulalongkorn, all hilltribes and minority groups were considered Thai subjects.[3] By the Thai Nationality Act of 1911 which gave Thai citizenship to all persons born in Thailand, nationality was recognized as essentially cultural and could include any ethnic group. The central government, which wanted a large population, encouraged their officials to enroll as many people as possible. Those that actually received citizenship papers, however, mainly lived in or near cities where the officials could reach them. Residents of more remote areas, beyond the reach of government officials, were generally (and basically unintentionally) left out. And although the Nationality Act could be applied to different ethnic groups, the hill people, such as those threatened with deportation in the 1921 incident over the police draft, were not sought out by Thai officials issuing citizenship papers. The fact that they settled in the hills, sometimes in areas deliberately hard for others to reach, further kept the number of highlander citizens low.

Since the hill people caused lowlanders few problems, they were left alone. Evicting them or preventing new in-migration was far too difficult for the Thai government to have attempted even if it had decided to do so. Many highland groups, particularly those growing opium, saw no advantage in being a Thai citizen and only rarely attempted to become one.

3. This did not include expatriate Chinese, Japanese, Indians, and Europeans residing in Thailand, who were considered aliens.

In the 1950s, when modern hilltribe policy first was being formulated, most hill people did not have citizenship. As non-Thais in border areas related to ethnic groups involved in insurgencies in other countries and often growing opium, they now came to be perceived as a security risk. Nevertheless until 1972, Thai citizenship remained available to all persons born in Thailand. This changed under the Revolutionary Party, a group of high-ranking military leaders under the leadership of Prime Minister Tanom Kittikachorn that consolidated their hold on power by dissolving Parliament in 1971. With the issuance of Revolutionary Party Order no. 337 in 1972, citizenship rights for persons whose paternal grandfather was not a Thai were severely restricted.[4]

Since the burden of proving one's ancestry fell on the hilltribes, the opportunity to become a Thai citizen for hilltribes, a significant portion of whom were not recent immigrants, declined significantly. In some cases, tribal people who had been Thai citizens but who could not prove that their paternal grandfather was Thai, had their citizenship revoked.

When a new, more liberal government took power in 1973, it decided to try to integrate those already in the country into the Thai civil order. New Ministry of Interior regulations on issuing the hilltribes Thai identity cards allowed immigrants

---

4. At that time, during the Vietnamese War in which Thailand had allied itself with the United States, the government had grown alarmed over the many Vietnamese immigrants in the northeast. To make it difficult for them to ingratiate themselves into society and looking to the day when they might be repatriated, Revolutionary Order No. 337 was promulgated to keep them from becoming Thai citizens. However, because the order was written vaguely, it applied throughout Thailand. Although the order could have been used to strip citizenship from persons of recent Chinese ancestry in Bangkok, officials enforced it most frequently with ethnic non-Thais such as Vietnamese in the northeast and hilltribes.

from Burma before 1975 and from Laos before 1976 to be eligible to join this process. Continued migration and the lack of alternatives in how to deal with these people frustrated these attempts, leading to a large number of people living in the country without papers.

More complicating factors remained. All Thai citizens must reside in legal villages. However, no legal villages can exist in forests which are, by Thai law, meant to be uninhabited. All Thai citizens must also be listed on a household registration (*thabian ban*). Even if they qualify for citizenship, if they cannot accomplish this, they are all but frustrated in acquiring the identity card that proves Thai citizenship and grants the privileges (such as health care) to which they are entitled. Regulations within the ministry that penalized officials who gave citizenship to individuals who later committed crimes served to hinder hilltribes from becoming Thai citizens.

By 1990, when opium production had been significantly reduced, far less than half the estimated 600,000 hill people were Thai citizens. Although changes in 2000 that give the district officer considerably more authority in granting citizenship have led to many hill people being naturalized, for decades, citizenship regulations constrained effective highland development work.

Linked with citizenship is the issue of loyalty. From the 1950s, Thai officials regularly doubted the loyalty of many hill people to the Thai government, often because of the insurgencies in neighboring countries. Occasionally, during the late 1960s and early 1970s, Hmong came into armed conflict with the Thai. Besides armed suppression of these uprisings, the government promoted the extension of Thai schools into the hills (often with Border Patrol Police as teachers). The modern Thai educational system, established in the early twentieth century to assimilate Chinese and other such groups into Thai life, has been extremely effective in making such people culturally Thai.

During the 1980s as the Thai educational system expanded into the hills, the younger generation of hill people began becoming Thai in the cultural sense. They learned the Thai language, along with Thai etiquette, Thai history, and all manner of things Thai until, in many cases, they came to appreciate Thai ways better than that of their own ethnic group. Together with exposure to mass media such as magazines and television, many young people were attracted to urban ways which they saw as Thai.

ALTERNATIVE CROPS

Since the poppy was only one commodity cultivated by most hill growers, the relation between the money they received for raw opium and their economic well-being varied. Also because opium yields fluctuated significantly depending on climatic changes, cash income from opium varied accordingly. Nevertheless, no crop could bring farmers more income per hectare than opium. Despite the occasional poor harvest, on the whole opium earned farmers 10,000–12,000 per hectare at that time.

The most popular alternative crop in the early 1970s was the peach. In the early 1970s, the indigenous peach sold for about 8 baht per kilogram, sufficient to earn villagers so satisfactory an income that some converted opium fields to peach tree cultivation. The attention given it by the UN Project and His Majesty the King contributed to its widespread cultivation which ironically also contributed to the farmgate price of peaches falling to about 2 baht per kilogram. Many growers did not even take their produce to market because the income would not even cover the cost of transportation (Lee 1981, p. 224).

Nevertheless, this experience taught project personnel that alternative sources of income besides opium cultivation

Ban Phui Hmong villagers collecting kidney bean seeds

Mae Sa Mai Hmong village marigolds on old opium field

existed. The experience also taught that securing a steady income from other sources was problematic. Sources first had to be identified. They had to be derived from activities in the highland village that did not duplicate produce in the lowlands. The crops or other items produced had to be something that could be accomplished by the technology existing in hill villages without electricity or other inputs including data, comprehensive training, and good roads. They had to be transportable to the lowlands in good condition. In many cases new markets had to be created in the lowlands so that the highland produce could be sold. Existing technology sometimes had to be modified to meet market demands. Quality control to meet market preferences was another important factor.

Experiences with three crops show the opportunities and troubles of introducing replacements for the opium poppy.

RED KIDNEY BEAN

Also known as red bean or haricort rouges, this variety of *phaseolus vulgaris*, of Central or South American origin, has a definite kidney shape. They were brought to Europe in the sixteenth century where they grew popular for use in salads. A factor in making them popular was that, because they ripen prior to harvest and are threshed dry from the pod, they can be stored for years in their mature dry form. Since the ancestral home of *phaseolus vulgaris* lay at the boundary of two climatic zones, subtropical dry and tropical temperate, the species was adaptable to a wide range of environments. The kidney bean, which also was used as tribute in the Aztec and Incan empires, attracted the attention of nineteenth-century European scientists who devoted considerable attention to improving it genetically. Kidney beans were not used in Thai cooking at all, however, and could only be found in some hotels and restaurants catering to Westerners.

Kidney beans found their way into Thai highland development through Richard Mann, an agricultural specialist who came to Thailand in 1959 to work with the American Baptist Mission in Chiang Mai.[1] He recognized in the kidney bean a flexible crop that could be grown in the Thai highlands but which required little special post-harvest care. To introduce the kidney bean to the Thai public and thus create a larger market for it, television features explained what it was and how it could be cooked.

The price offered by the UN opium replacement project in 1973 for kidney beans was about 3 baht per kilogram. A 1975 UNFDAC report estimated that the hill people sold 10 tons of beans to buyers other than the project that would represent an income to the growers of approximately 30,000 baht. In the early years, the use of an imported hybrid seed initially required growers to purchase seed each year. The project decided to distribute kidney bean seeds on a wider scale and the crop has now been well established (UNFDAC 1975 Annex 4, p. 5). Although there were areas where kidney bean cultivation failed, such as Khun Wang (Lee 1981, pp. 223–224), the bean is now found throughout the country in major supermarkets and has been integrated into various Thai dishes as well.

---

1. He served as senior advisor to HAMP, TN-HDP, and later ran the Projects Coordination Office in Chiang Mai in the early 1990s. Later he worked in drug rehabilitation with the Karen and Hmong in Bo Kaeo, Chiang Mai.

CABBAGE

Cabbage, which developed in northern Europe millenia ago prior to the Aryan invasion, was known to the Greeks. Head cabbage (*Brassica oleracea var. Capitata*), the most important type, was developed in the Middle Ages. Cabbage grows best in temperate climates; if temperatures are too high, quality will be adversely affected. Cabbage seems to have been spread to Southeast Asia by the Arabs (cabbage was not mentioned in the Bible and thus probably was unknown to the Hebrews). The Thai word for cabbage, *kalampli*, seems to be derived from the Arab word, *krombe*.

Cabbage came to be used widely throughout rural Thailand by the nineteenth century if not much earlier. Its spread to the hills, however, occurred only in the 1960s. At that time, a road from Hot district in Chiang Mai was being built westward to Mae Sariang district of Mae Hong Son province. The deputy director general of the Highway Department grew some cabbage near Mae Ho, about ten kilometers east of Mae Sariang so the workers would have a source of green vegetables to eat. Karens in the area observed this and began growing some themselves (Wanat interview 1997). From here it spread to Hmong living in Mae Tho, the opium-growing village studied by Geddes and one of the first UNFDAC project sites.

It was not the projects, however, that promoted the cabbage but the Hmong themselves. In the late 1970s farmers could earn one baht per head from cabbage. As many as 60,000 head could be packed into single hectare plots resulting in income far greater than the same for opium (Chavalit interview 2000). However, to obtain these yields, chemical pesticides and fertilizers had to be applied that resulted in water pollution and potential harm to the growers. As a result, UN and other development projects chose other crops to promote. In some places, such as in Pa Kluai, in Chiang Mai's Chom Thong District, in the area of the Thai-Norwegian Church Aid Highland Development Project, conflicts occurred between Hmong cabbage growers and the lowland Thai in the 1980s that have not been resolved (Renard 1994).

Recognizing the earnings they could gain from cabbage at about the same time as opium eradication began in the mid 1980s, many Hmong turned to raising cabbage. Using techniques learned from development projects, they introduced chemical pesticides, gravity-fed sprinklers, and stone retaining walls. Where one could have seen opium poppies from one hill to the next in Mae Tho, one could now see cabbage heads. By 1990, ten-wheeled trucks were driving to Mae Tho, Pa Kluai, and other cabbage growing centers to purchase tons of the vegetable for overnight shipment to Bangkok, Phuket, and elsewhere.

The income earned by the larger entrepreneurs was substantial. In a vegetable marketing survey by Payap University, the average price in northern Thailand for cabbage from 1982 –1985 averaged about 4.5 baht (Anusorn et al. 1986, p. 43). The yield for a rai with 60,000 head would thus have been 270,000 baht (over $10,000 at the time) and this plot could have been replanted more than once every year. Profits reached millions of baht for successful growers, sufficient to propel them into a lifestyle of suburban houses with big cars and expensive education for their children.

At the same time, vitriolic controversies flared over the pollution of streams flowing into lowland villages. Irate valley dwellers, ethnic Thais mostly, have carried out protests for over a decade that have sometimes included walks on Government House in Bangkok, roadblocks of major highways, and burning in effigy professors at Chiang Mai University who were seen as supporting the hill people. These protests have sometimes included calls for the non-Thai aliens to be pushed out of Thailand but no avail. Even though the director-general of the Royal Forest Department in the late-1980s said that Pa Kluai would be the first village in Thailand to be relocated, the village is still there.

COFFEE

The coffee bean is a species in the madder family known as *Caffea Arabica*. Originating in eastern Africa in and around Ethiopia, coffee spread slowly eastward reaching Southeast Asia in about the seventeenth century. The *Robusta* variety of coffee came to be cultivated in the south of Thailand but even in the mid twentieth century coffee was not nearly as popular as tea in the country.

Coffee was among the first crops tried by the UN in northern Thailand where the *arabica* variety was introduced. By 1974, thousands of coffee seedlings had been distributed. Although many died or became diseased, the Hmong in Khun Wang, and presumably elsewhere, continued to show interest in cultivating the crop (Lee 1981, pp. 229–233).

In promoting coffee, the UN projects recognized the importance of the guaranteed world market for the product that would avoid problems of price fluctuations such as with the indigenous peach. The Dutch supported a coffee project in Chiang Mai with an office at Chiang Mai University. The Swiss food giant, Nestlé, offered 60 baht a kilogram for coffee encouraging many to start coffee growing. There were some outstanding successes with some growers at Doi Chang in Chiang Rai earning $10,000–15,000 in a single year (Beno interview 2000).

However, coffee production placed demands on the growers. At the beginning of cultivation, three years lead time was

General Chavalit (second from left) and Richard Mann (foreground)
with coffee trees

required before harvesting the first crop. This meant the farmers needed land security and confidence they could stay in the same place that long. Second, coffee requires processing in the village by the grower to meet market grading requirements to get the guaranteed price. Third, tending the coffee trees and protecting them from pests and diseases was something new for the hill people. They also had to learn how to grade coffee and other techniques.

These demands have proven so onerous for many that they have largely stopped growing coffee. Despite the successes at places like Doi Chang and the enthusiastic recommendation by the village leaders there that other opium growers shift to coffee growing, this seems to be the exception rather than the rule. The Royal Project no longer promotes it because project management believes the growing requirements are too high to be viable in village conditions (Suthat interview 2000). They suggest that except in unusual circumstances coffee in northern Thailand can only be productively grown in plantation conditions such as is done on Doi Tung.

CUT FLOWERS

It would not be until later, about 1990, that cut flowers were developed as a crop that villagers could grow readily and also for which a good market existed. Estimates of the maximum yield of cut flowers ran as high as 200,000 baht per hectare (Chavalit interview 2000). Although some chemical inputs are needed, they are far less than cabbage, making this a desirable crop to many. The Royal Project has identified cut flowers as being the best crop the hill people can grow for sale in the marketplace at present (Suthat interview 2000).

ECONOMIC AND SOCIAL WELL-BEING

Prices for alternative crops are not the only significant factor. As planners have gradually realized that economic evaluations of development have limitations (Enters 1992), new conceptions have been formulated regarding what crops should be grown and what approaches taken to replace opium. There are factors sometimes more important than price to be considered, as the farmers in Pa Kluai have learned. While the Royal Project is promoting the use of food crops, because they offer the farmer food on which to subsist as well as income generation, not all crops (such as cabbage) may be socially acceptable. Other values have come to be applied, such as the ability to make a living in one's village by growing food crops. Through the thirty years of work, the objectives of the undertaking grew more holistic.

Changes are being made in how social and economic indicators are compiled. When the practice of using such indicators began, proponents hoped that economic indicators, such as GNP, could be used to predict the future state of the economy. Later this was expanded to include certain social indicators such as age expectancy to predict the future standard of living. Proponents expected that the benefits from economic growth would trickle down to the poor and that society as a whole would progress. However, variability in how long it took the indicators to have the expected impact and various "false signals" frustrated the economic planners from being able to predict future economic activity. Also, purely economic indicators do not recognize the intrinsic value of an activity, making it difficult to identify ways to improve the quality of life.

To overcome these shortcomings, social scientists became involved in an effort to devise a model of "well-being." Although there are ongoing debates over what "well-being" means, most definitions refer to various physical conditions that influence a person's ability to survive as well as to reproduce. Longevity, good health, and other such factors are being incorporated in various definitions of well-being.

Thailand, in preparing the Ninth Plan, has recognized the importance of well-being indicators. Particularly after the crash of its booming economy in 1997 and the ensuing financial crisis, government planners reevaluated their approach. Building on the people-centered Eighth Plan, they began identifying new indicators that went beyond the more purely economic indicators of the past.

Two major projects in Thailand have taken the lead in this initiative. The first was organized by the NESDB with support from the Asian Development Bank. The second is run by Chulalongkorn University's Social Research Institute with support from the Thailand Research Fund. The former project builds on the work of Nobel Prize winner, A. K. Sen, who wrote that development, like freedom, requires economic facilities, social opportunity, and protective security. The latter project has identified eight main groups of indicators: infrastructure and environment; occupational and economic; health; education and human resource development; information and media; cultural and spiritual; civil society; and good governance. These are being tested in nine different locations within Thailand including an upland cultivation area (UNDP 1999, p. 177). UNDP's present definition of development is the "process of enlarging people's choices to live long and healthy lives, to have access to knowledge, and to have access to income and assets: to enjoy a decent standard of living."

Because of these changes, applying the data collected by the development projects in the 1970s and 1980s by using the well-being model is problematic. However, in order to provide some indication of overall conditions in the 1970s, an effort to assess conditions in the hills three decades ago will be

Table 6
POVERTY INDICATORS AMONG THAI HIGHLANDERS IN THE 1960s

INDICATOR	SITUATION IN 1960s
1. Community Participation 2. Women's Organizations 3. Community Savings and Loan Groups 4. Sharing of Knowledge through Livelihood Groups and Networks 5. Diligent Attitude to Livelihood Activities 6. Environmental Protection	1. High participation in traditional clan groups 2. None 3. None 4. Within village and clans high, but otherwise no such groups existed 5. High 6. Opium growers expected to move on to new fertile fields after exhausting fields by intensive cultivation; but among other groups like Karens, high concern for environmental protection
7. Less Capital Intensive Forms of Agriculture.	7. Opium only major cash crop but trading cartels provided capital and other inputs, bought crop.
8. Subsistence Farming	8. High (even for most opium growers).

made. This will follow the common country assessment model used by the United Nations Resident Coordinator System in 1999. This system identified eight indicators of success in overcoming socioeconomic constraints associated with poverty (UNDP 1999, p. 4).

The development process began with the promotion of capital-intensive crops with less attention initially to subsistence crops. By the second phase of development, however, the projects were working, at a time when these indicators had not been identified formally, in fact to fulfill all of them.

New organizations, including credit groups and village funds, activity groups, and networks (such as textile-weaving cooperatives) were established by government and internationally funded projects. Time was required to popularize and strengthen them. The role of women in agriculture was recognized soon and steps taken accordingly. For example, when projects held training meetings, conventionally men attended even though the women were actively involved in working the fields. Transfer of information from the trainers to the women was sometimes incomplete, resulting in problems, such as misuse of pesticides, which harmed the women's health. Women trainers who could speak tribal languages then became part of the training process. Efforts were made to transfer the diligent attitude towards traditional work to the new activities. In this regard, General Chavalit suggests that projects should choose to work only with the diligent individuals so that they can set a good example for others (interview 2000). The projects, in introducing new agricultural methods, found the highland environment fragile and different than the lowlands. Time and considerable experimentation was required before appropriate cropping systems were identified. Finally, subsistence crop production was promoted more in the final decade (Suthat interview 2000).

THE EVOLUTION OF APPROACHES TO OPIUM ERADICATION

Opium poppy replacement and the development work supporting it, scanned three decades and comprised three phases. During the 1970s, initiatives were established to replace the poppy with other crops. When the difficulty of this became clear, a second phase of rural integrated development projects was carried out that coincided approximately with the 1980s. The final phase was reached in the 1990s when demand reduction and community-based participatory work were recognized as being essential to the process. In phase 3, the work can properly be called alternative development. The phases were:

1. Early initiatives involving crop replacement (1970s)
2. Rural Integrated Development (late 1970s to late 1980s)
3. Participatory Alternative Development (1990 to present)

The evolution of these three phases is discussed below. Reference is made to national socioeconomic and political developments, important trends in UN work, and other pertinent events. Problems are reviewed with special attention as to how they were dealt with and how they contributed to later work.

Table 7

MAJOR ROYAL, UN, AND BILATERAL HIGHLAND DEVELOPMENT PROJECTS IN NORTHERN THAILAND [a]

PROJECT	DONORS	BUDGET (million US$)	AGENCY	YEARS	PROVINCES
Royal Projects	Various	100 (approx)	Royal Household	1969–present	All northern provinces
Doi Tung Highland Development Project	Various	25	Mae Fah Luang Foundation	1988–present	Chiang Rai
Thai Agricultural Research Services Project	USA	n/a	Royal Project	1973–ca 1985	All northern provinces
Thai/UN Crop Replacement and Community Development Project	USA, UN	3.4[b]	UNFDAC/ONCB	1972–1979	Chiang Mai, Chiang Rai
Thai/UN Highland Area Marketing and Production Project	n/a	3.7[b]	ONCB	1979–1984	Chiang Mai
Mae Sa Integrated Watershed Development Project	Netherlands	3.0	RFD	1973–1981	Chiang Mai
Highland Coffee Research and Development Centre	USA (USAID)	1.5	CMU	1982–1992	Chiang Mai
Mae Chaem Integrated Watershed Development Project	USA (USAID)	9.0	Chiang Mai Prov.	1980–1989	Chiang Mai
Hill Areas Education Project	Germany (GTZ)	1.5	NFED	1980–1986	Chiang Mai, Chiang Rai, Lampang
Thai-German Highland Development Programme	USA	25.0	ONCB	1981–present	Chiang Mai, Chiang Rai, Mae Hong Son
Narcotics Crop Cultivation Control Project	Australia (AIDAB)	5.0 (approx)	ONCB 3rd Army PWD	ca. 1980–90	6 northern provinces
Thai-Australia Highland Agricultural and Social Development Project		8.0[c] (approx)		1986–1993[c]	Key villages in 6 northern provinces

Project	Donor	Funding[a]	Thai agency	Years	Location
Thai/UN Norwegian Church Aid Highland Development Project	Norwegian Church Aid Norway	6.0[b]	PWD	1985–1992	Chiang Mai, Lampang Phayao, Chiang Rai
Thai/UN Pae Por Highland Development Project	Sweden	2.5[b]	DOLA	1986–1994	Chiang Mai, Tak
Thai/UN Doi Sam Mun Highland Development Project	Canada and Sweden	3.5[b]	RFD	1987–1994	Chiang Mai
Thai/UN Wiang Pha Highland Development Project	Intl. Order of Good Templars	2.9[b]	RFD	1987–1994	Chiang Mai
Thai/WIF Highland Development Project	Norway	1.5[b] (approx)	ONCB	1987–1994	All northern provinces
Thai/New Zealand Cooperative Temperate Fruit Tree Development Project	New Zealand	0.5 (approx)	MOA	1989–1992	Chiang Mai, Chiang Rai, Lamphun
Thai/UN Doi Yao-Pha Mon Highland Development Project	Japan	0.7[c]	ONCB	1990–1994	Nan
Thai/UN Integrated Pocket Area Development Project	Germany	3.9[b]	ONCB, Chiang Mai, Mae Hong Son	1990–1994	Chiang Mai and Mae Hong Son
Thai/UN Strengthening of Community-Based Drug Prevention Strategies in the Highlands of Northern Thailand		0.27[d]	ONCB	1994–1996	Chiang Mai

[a] In millions of U.S. dollars based on bilateral or UN donor contributions (the Thai government provided additional inputs in kind and in cash).

[b] UNFDAC n.d; UNDCP 1994; Williams 1979; Anek and Suwannarat 1994.

[c] Continuation of Thai-Australia-World Bank Land Dev. Proj (1980–1986, US$11.1) AIDAB: Australian International Development Assistance Board

[d] UNDCP Regional Centre, Bangkok.

CMU: Chiang Mai University

DOLA: Department of Local Administration, Ministry of Interior

GTZ: German Agency for Technical Cooperation

HADF: Hill Area Development Foundation (NGO)

MOA: Ministry of Agriculture

NFED: Nonformal Education Department, Ministry of Education

NNCC: Northern Narcotic Control Center (Chiang Mai)

ONCB: Office of Narcotics Control Board, Office of the Prime Minister

PWD: Public Welfare Department Ministry of Interior (as of 1995 Labor and Social Welfare)

RFD: Royal Forest Department, Ministry of Agriculture

UN: United Nations

UNDCP: United Nations International Drug Control Programme

UNFDAC: United Nations Fund for Drug Abuse Control

WIF: Worldview International Foundation (Norway)

Figure 1
OPIUM CULTIVATION AREAS IN NORTHERN THAILAND (1999–2000)

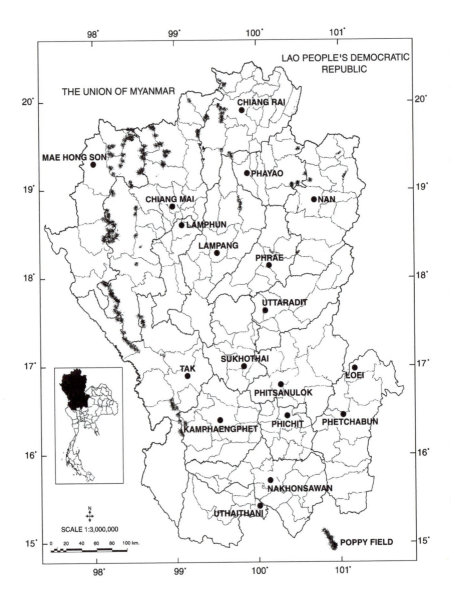

EARLY CROP REPLACEMENT INITIATIVES

Highland development work in Thailand during the 1970s aimed to replace opium with other cash crops. The earliest programs were sponsored by the royal family arising out of King Bhumibol Adulyadej's own personal interest in the welfare of these people. The king recognized that the growing problem in the hills endangered national security as well as the welfare of the hill people. He expanded the scope of his general humanitarian activities to include assistance to the hilltribes.

Since his first trip to Chiang Mai in 1958, and the construction of the Bhubing Rachaniwet Palace in 1962 high on Doi Suthep to the west of the city, the king had met hill people, learning of their cultures and backgrounds. He saw the generally unrewarded efforts to resettle hilltribes in the lowlands at so-called *nikhom* beginning in the years 1960–1963. He was dismayed by the United Nations project preparation mission that estimated annual opium production in Thailand at 145 tons as well as the increasing number of incidents between Thai army and police units and people in the hills.

The royal family had begun working directly with people in rural areas since the early 1960s. In 1966 a *Nuai Phraratcha-than* (Royal Assistance Unit) was established which then made seven trips to southern Thailand. For the eighth trip, in December of 1969, they went north. His Majesty already met the Hmong at Doi Pui village, a few kilometers beyond Bhubing Palace. In 1968, he found, as had UN socioeconomic survey team members earlier, that opium growers made money from multiple sources. When he learned of the income earned from the indigenous peach, the king thought that grafting an improved variety onto the local rootstock would yield better

King Bhumibol Adulyadej observing indigenous peach

fruit (*Royal Project* 1995, p. 17). In the king's words, the Royal Project began this way:

> I asked the Meos [at Doi Pui] how much a family earned in average from the annual selling of opium. The answer was 3,000 to 5,000 Baht. When asked how much the annual selling of fruits would bring, the reply was that local variety of peaches would bring 4,000 to 12,000 Baht! It was then that we thought we had the answer. We could improve the wild fruits, such as local peaches, by grafting. We could also choose other fruits which are high-priced and in great demand, such as apples, pears, and chestnuts. In fact, there is a great number of wild trees and other plants that could be used, including some medicinal herbs. These present no marketing problem. And the hill-tribe will not have to compete with the lowland as the crops cannot be successfully grown there (Royal Address and Speeches 1970, p. 40).

To find which improved variety would be best and to overcome the absence of Thai expertise on highland farming, the king instituted the Royal Project in 1969. He provided on-the-spot help in the tribal villages, teaching farming and marketing techniques as well as conducting research. The first training program was held in 1970 to prepare representatives of fifteen tribal villages in agricultural extension (Aran 1976, p. 46). King Bhumibol Adulyadej then established the Doi Ang Khang Highland Development Station in the north of Chiang Mai province to test the viability of agricultural alternatives to the opium poppy. Other stations, such as at Chang Khian, on Doi Suthep, and close to Bhubing Palace were also set up.

An excerpt from the notes taken by Princess Vibhavadi Rangsit indicates clearly the concern the king had for the hill people (Sadet Doi 1970).

Their majesties flew by Royal helicopter to the village of Mae Sa Mai. . . . This Maeo village has a population of 118 White and Green Maeo. His Majesty distributed iodized salt and gave Rhode Island Red roosters to the villagers. Their Majesties also gave cotton cloth and clothing and candy to the villagers as well as notebooks and pencils to the 44 schoolchildren. In addition they gave tick medication and a medicine locker to the village headman. His Majesty then visited the peach orchard and the pigpen containing the boar he had donated the previous year, whose piglets were now running around the village. When His Majesty suggested that the villagers use sorghum as pig feed, the headman said that pigs don't eat sorghum. When His Majesty picked up some sorghum and offered it, the pigs lapped it up. The headman was immediately delighted. . . . One White Maeo woman who could speak Thai well came to see Her Majesty and sang a song. In the village, the physicians in the royal party examined and treated 82 persons. Children in general suffered from malnutrition and from eye disease. Many adults had goiter.

King Bhumibol Adulyadej contributed to highland development work in other ways. Among the most influential was his guideline that opium poppies not be destroyed until viable alternatives existed. The king realized that the radical removal of the hill people's source of income would imperil them.

Most officials working in hills during the early 1970s thought this would not take long. They believed that the poppy was essentially a lucrative but illegal crop that could be replaced with relative ease. Pushed by Egil Krogh's promise of American financial support for quick action, Thai and UN project planners rushed to start work and achieve results.

These officials realized they knew nothing about the Thai uplands. They knew that no one in the entire country had experience in opium poppy replacement. According to Narong Suwwanapiam, who worked in the hills since 1977, entering the highlands was almost like going to another country. For a graduate of political science from Chulalongkorn University in Bangkok, the cultural differences between people like him and the Hmong and others were immense (Narong, interview).

The spirit of the earliest projects was to achieve results at all costs. When government officials recognized that some Thai laws and regulations governing hill people were inadequate, and more applicable in the lowlands, they sought ad hoc solutions. When roads had to be built or special equipment acquired, ways were found to get the job done inside or outside the system.

Ad hoc solutions were needed because no single Thai agency was (or is) responsible for the hills as a whole. Many agencies, such as the Public Welfare Department, the Bureau of Narcotic Drugs (after 1976, incorporated into the newly estab-

Queen Sirikit at Pha Mi Akha village, Chiang Rai

Queen Sirikit at Border Police school, Pha Mi Akha village

lished Office of Narcotics Control Board), and the Royal Forest Department, worked in the hills, often with overlapping mandates. These agencies were only nominally beholden to National Tribal Committees, which had little real authority. International agencies implementing highland projects were generally obliged to work with one counterpart agency accentuating inter-agency rivalries. As a result, activities outside the direct responsibility of the agency that was assigned to the project proceeded slowly.

Finding suitable replacement cash crops for the lucrative and adaptive opium poppy was difficult. Despite early hopes that suitable crops could be readily identified, opium replacement met many obstacles. Low market prices, crop pests, the lack of credit for highland growers, poor transportation and packaging facilities, as well as the unfamiliarity of certain crops to lowland buyers all frustrated crop replacement efforts.

There was one misconception that hindered work not related directly to crop replacement. This was the mistaken belief that opium users could be rehabilitated relatively easily through short courses in lowland detoxification centers. It was found, however, that when detoxified addicts returned to the hills, over 90 percent relapsed, often because of pressure from their friends who had not sought treatment. Many hill people were detoxified more than once only to relapse again.

People's participation, or the lack of it, was an important factor. Personnel of all the early initiatives stated that their projects were people oriented. In a report on the Crop Replacement and Community and Development Project (CRCDP 1979, p. 2), the UNFDAC program director, I. M. G. Williams, noted that "the co-operation of the opium poppy growers from project villages was won." The leadership of the Thai/UN Highland Agricultural Marketing and Production Project (HAMP), which followed CRCDP and other early projects, were also convinced they had won the people's support.

Paul Lewis, an American missionary fluent in Akha and Lahu who had worked with these groups in Myanmar and Thailand since the late 1940s, offered a different opinion. Regarding HAMP, he wrote:

> The tribal people themselves were not brought in at the planning stage. The program was brought to them, with the general attitude, "Aren't you lucky! Look at the wonderful goodies we are bringing to you." If they found that any villagers did not like what they proposed they sometimes talked them into accepting it one way or another (Lewis 1985 pp. 27–28).
>
> How much better it would be to discuss every aspect of the problem with tribal leaders from the VERY START [emphasis in the original]. . . . For those who are upset by this suggestion, it might be well to ponder: "Has the method of excluding the tribal people worked?" (Lewis 1985 pp. 26, 25).

Yet it should be remembered that the model for development in the Thai system was top-down in the extreme. The government determined all infrastructure development from roads to schools. Community development followed this approach. When the village of Ku Daeng in Saraphi district of Chiang Mai province was identified as a "model development village" in 1967, government officials told the villagers what committees to establish and provided virtually all the inputs for agricultural and other improvements (Kingshill 1991, pp. 103–104). Despite the truth of what Lewis was saying, the CRCDP officials were cooperating with the villagers far more than Thai officials customarily did in lowland villages. Observed an NGO activist, Chatchawan Thongdiloet, "the role of the villagers in this system was only to cooperate . . . according to the directives of the state" (Chatchawan 2001).

All those in the early projects learned. The officials learned about the hills and crops that could grow there. Opium growers, who mostly only knew lowland officials as soldiers or police who came to fight or arrest them, learned there were Thai officials with whom they could cooperate. General Chavalit remembered the hard work it took to overcome the hill people's hatred for the police when they first began crop replacement work (Chavalit interview). Working at a time of sporadic ethnic insurgency in northern Thailand, the project officials faced many challenges in gaining entry into highland villages.

CROP REPLACEMENT AND COMMUNITY DEVELOPMENT PROJECT (CRCDP)

Quick problem solving and high ideal characterized the CRCDP. As the first UNFDAC development project, the first problem it had to solve was reaching an arrangement with the United Nations Development Programme, which was the UN's largest agency as well as the development arm of the organization. Jealous of the agency's prerogatives regarding UNFDAC which had been established only in 1969, UNDP officials in Bangkok sought to control the project's management and dictate its direction.

Red tape within the UN was cut by making the UNFDAC the implementing agency for CRCDP, the first crop replacement project in the world. Having Lisalotte Waldheim, the daughter of UN Secretary General Kurt Waldheim, at the program office in UNFDAC headquarters facilitated project implementation.

Red tape in Thailand was cut because Prince Bhisadej Rajani, director of the Royal Project, was named project manager. For several years, cooperation was so strong between CRCDP and the Royal Project that they functioned almost as one (Mann 2000). The Royal Project had begun operations in 1969, was already carrying out opium poppy replacement, and had learned lessons from which CRCDP would later profit.

The CRCDP was officially established in an agreement signed by the UN and Thailand on 7 December 1971 (CRCDP 1973, p. 2). The Thai counterpart agency was the Bureau of Narcotic Drugs, largely an enforcement agency and located within the Royal Thai Police Department. With assistance from the Food and Agriculture Organization, CRCDP was to replace opium with other cash crops and promote the additional cultivation of food crops.

In its seven-year lifetime, the CRCDP established the Chang Khian Field Crop Development Station on a former Hmong village where opium had been grown. Two Thai fruit and nut experimental centers known collectively as the Doi Pui Temperate Fruit and Nut Experimental Station were also established on former opium-growing sites on Doi Suthep mountain, west of Chiang Mai. The project also supported work at the Ang Khang Highland Development Station in Chiang Mai province.

Primary activities were carried out at five key villages representing Hmong, Lisu, and Yunnanese Chinese. From these key villages, activities reached out to an additional twenty-five "satellite" villages throughout northern Thailand. Dozens of varieties of cash crops were tested. Although opium reduction was not an immediate objective in this project, and fields and production were not measured, still, one key and one satellite village were declared opium free by 1979 (Williams 1979, p. 34).

CRCDP Director I. M. G. Williams (third from left),
Richard Mann (fourth from left), staff, and villagers

During the project, planners recognized the many issues surrounding poppy replacement that had to be resolved. The project manager's 1979 report read that "an integrated community development programme is the course to follow." Williams envisioned a wider program incorporating treatment and rehabilitation, primary health care, and other services together with crop replacement. Through such means it would be more possible he noted to detect "possible future heroin addiction" (Williams 1979, pp. 38–39). This approach would also enable the new project to deal with issues such as land tenure, which as the UN consultant noted in 1967 could turn the "hill people . . . [into] outlaws at any moment" (1967, p. 540).

Another problem was that sometimes the project did not buy the crops that it had promoted. As documented by the Hmong anthropologist Lee, several growers in Khun Wang village, Chiang Mai province complained that project officials reneged on their promises several times in the mid 1970s which dampened their initial enthusiasm for the UNFDAC project. To be more effective, Lee suggested that the project would have to change its focus "to be in line with the people's needs and the reality of their habitat" (Lee 1981, pp. 221–223, 272).[1]

Much of the Thai staff was young, idealistic, and enthused about participating in this new venture. Belonging to the generation of young people who toppled the Thai government on 14 October 1973, they felt their work developing the hills was contributing to the future stability of the country. They saw it as a positive alternative to the insurgencies that had been growing in hill areas since the 1960s.

On entering villages, their first priority was to befriend the villagers, to overcome suspicion where it existed and replace it with trust. The first generation of project officials ignored opium cultivation and engaged in no suppression. Narong told how they sometimes tried indirect means to reduce opium cultivation such as promoting cash crop cultivation in opium fields. Richard Mann noted, "I will never forget the remarks of the Australian ambassador during a helicopter trip to Doi Sam Mun, Chiang Mai province, when he asked: 'Why has opium poppy been planted in that coffee field?' I answered: 'opium poppy was not planted in that coffee field; coffee was planted in that poppy field'" (Mann personal communication).

The time-consuming process by which these obstacles were dealt with, if not actually overcome in the 1970s, provided lessons for all. The issues faced in the early initiatives were so complex and unprecedented that all those involved were

1. But the CRCDP did buy beans and other crops planted in opium fields. Richard Mann, on the CRCDP staff, wrote that "crops interplanted with the poppy such as red kidney beans, coffee, and cabbage were . . . purchased by CRCDP (Mann personal communication 2000).

Figure 2
MAP OF MAJOR HIGHLAND PROJECTS

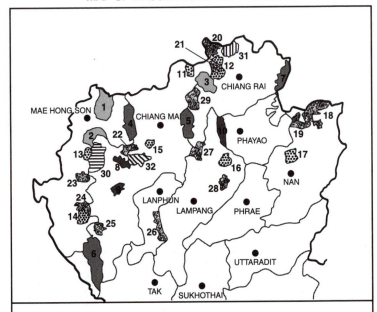

| | TG-HDP | | TA-HASD PROJECT PHASE 1 | | | 30. mae Chaem WDP |

TG-HDP

1. Huai Phuling
2. Pang Mapha
3. Tambon Wawi

TA-HASD PROJECT PHASE 1

11. Lo Pa Khrai
12. Mae Chan
13. Hua Phon
14. Mae Chang
15. Mae Ta Man
16. Mae Mi
17. Mae Khaning

30. mae Chaem WDP

UN PROJECTS

4. Doi Sam Mun
5. Wiang Pha
6. Pae Po
7. Doi Yao-Pha Mon

PHASE 2

18. Thung Chang
19. Chiang Klang
20. Huai mae Kum
21. Huai Lu
22. Khun Sap
23. Huai Phung
24. Mae Rit Pa kae
25. Thung Loi
26. Thung Hua Chang
27. Mae Mi
28. Mae San
29. Mae Suai

31. Doi Tung HDP

32. Mae Sa WDP

TN HDP

8. Mon Ya
9. Khao San Aen
10. Pha Daeng

LEGEND

● PROVINCE
— INTER BOUNDARY
— PROV. BOUNDARY

N

unprepared to deal with them. Nevertheless, the considerable time, money, and effort invested by so many in dealing with highland drug problems yielded certain positive results.

THAI/UN HIGHLAND AGRICULTURAL MARKETING AND PRODUCTION PROJECT (HAMP)

In 1979, the Thai/UN Highland Agricultural Marketing and Production Project (HAMP) succeeded CRCDP in 18 of the former project villages. During its five year life, HAMP followed the CRCDP model with the objective of "bringing under control the drug abuse problem . . . by the progressive elimination of opium poppy cultivation" (HAMP 1984, p. vi). HAMP worked in three major opium producing areas: Omkoi and Chom Thong districts of Chiang Mai province and Wang Nua district in Lampang province.

Despite the report by the CRCDP project manager, Williams, calling for integrated watershed development, HAMP focussed more narrowly on agricultural research, extension, and production, marketing the crops grown under the project, and making agricultural credit available. The main innovation was a marketing component to find ways to sell the cash crops generated by CRCDP activities. HAMP continued field-testing potential replacement crops, thus providing later projects much information and experience. Activities were carried out in villages, of the major highland groups: initially Hmong, Karen, Lisu, Lahu, and Yunnanese Chinese and then, later, the Yao. Basic community infrastructure development such as roads, domestic water systems, and health centers that facilitated cash and, secondarily, food crop production were also provided. Besides some road building to facilitate the marketing of cash crops, HAMP devoted little attention to infrastructure development or issues of citizenship which, planners have hoped, would be solved through existing government channels. But as HAMP's final report noted that "in selected highland areas and on a limited scale, land certificates entitling families to farm small holdings are being issued" (HAMP 1984, p. 11), the issue was not ignored. Less attention was focussed on drug treatment or prevention. Everything was secondary to work on agricultural development and marketing to replace opium which remained the paramount and urgent goal as it had been since of Egil Krogh's visit to Chiang Mai.

This disproportionate favoring of agricultural development over the other important issues of highland development hindered progress. Not surprisingly, HAMP's final report states that opium replacement was "particularly difficult."[2] In 1981–1982, 3.85 metric tons of opium were grown in HAMP villages. Although in the last growing season of the project's life (1983–1984), production declined to 2.73 tons, it was poor weather that caused yield to decline from 8.875 to 7.257 kilograms/hectare. The area cultivated declined only from 39,200 hectares in 1980 to 36,800 hectares in 1984 (HAMP 1984, annex 11).

Part of the reason for opium's continued cultivation was the difficulty identifying suitable replacement crops.[3] Although coffee, red kidney bean, lettuce, and wheat seemed promising cash earners that were also socially acceptable, the income farmers derived from them was less than from opium

2. An observation confirmed by Lee (1981, p. 246): the UNFDAC project, he said, did not greatly benefit the Hmong economy: "There is no evidence of any noticeable substitution of opium with the—crops advanced to the Hmong by project workers."

3. The development projects did not promote cabbage, the commercial production of which was pioneered by the Hmong.

which explains the continued reliance on opium in Hmong and Yao villages, like Pa Kluai in Chom Thong district and Mae Sa Mai in Mae Rim district of Chiang Mai province as well as Mae San in Lampang province. What was lacking too was the integrated approach sought by Williams. As Richard Mann noted (personal communication 2000), high-ranking project officials were not "really concerned how the growers were coping and what short and long term effects the departure of the projects would have on them." The evidence was in the opium poppies in the fields.

THAI ARS CROP SUBSTITUTION PROGRAM

Additional American funding for crop replacement came in 1973 when the Agricultural Research Service of the United States Department of Agriculture began sponsoring research projects to find ways of identifying and developing "agricultural enterprises" that would "replace income lost by cessation of opium poppy growing" (Research Review Team 1977, p. ii). This project was overseen by the new Highland Agricultural Research Coordinating Committee under Prince Bhisatej Rajani, director of the Royal Project.

By 1979, nineteen research projects on crop substitution had been conducted often by university researchers in cooperation with the research stations established under the Royal Project or UN-sponsored work. Besides examining specific crops such as ornamentals, pyrethrum, tea, and coffee, studies examined essential oils, lac, conservation farming, silkworm cultivation, and apiculture (raising bees). Most researchers were from Kasetsart University. Food crop production was also supported. An experimental station on upland rice established in Samoeng district of Chiang Mai has since been taken over by the Ministry of Agriculture. When the ARS work came to an end in 1987, it had served as a link between the Royal Project and the United Nations projects as well as other highland initiatives in a vast amount of highland crop research.

NEW DIRECTIONS

The research on crop substitutes identified viable species. But even the best varieties identified were only partially successful. Although coffee earned high prices, the volatile international coffee market complicated the introduction of this crop. The market for kidney bean was still being created while cabbage was not yet widely cultivated in 1980. Substitute crop successes occurred erratically, depending on special conditions ranging from favorable weather, comprehensive agricultural extension, and individual initiative.

By the early 1980s, wider initiatives were being designed for implementation in the hills. The narrow focus on crop replacement was coming to an end. This showed that Thai officials were learning the actual problems in the hills and establishing programs to deal with them.

The work proceeded easier with the reduction in insurgent activity. Disagreements between factions within the student movement disillusioned many students who had fled to the jungles in 1976. Some important leaders emerged during the premiership of General Kriengsak. In a symbolic reconciliation in 1980, many were feted by the general at Ban Hin Taek (the former base of Khun Sa) with servings of his renowned brandied chicken curry.

The narrow focus of work and the difficulty in identifying suitable alternatives also gave rise to critics to the program. A few, such as Lee and Lewis, pointed to errors made in implementation, a lack of people's participation, as well as the difficulty in finding suitable alternatives. Others saw the entire package of highland activities, from suppressing the insurgencies, to relocating highlanders, delineating forest reserves, and replacing opium, as part of a larger undertaking to repress the indigenous peoples in the hills. Linked in many minds to the confusion over the Tribal Research Centre, the highland work took on negative connotations to many observers. Scholars, while often agreeing to serve as consultants for various projects, tended to avoid studying the process in their academic work.

Persons within the development community felt these pressures. The move to integrated rural development projects in the hills began to include the entire range of activities associated with improving the people's standard of living. While one main reason these projects existed at all in certain sites was to replace opium, the critique of the earlier opium replacement efforts and the negative publicity surrounding the efforts resulted in projects which made virtually no mention of opium replacement at all even though the poppy was grown within their project areas. Not only was opium cultivation downplayed; so too was the rehabilitation of opium users and preventive education about other substances.

Thai planners, less affected by the criticisms of the projects, also favored the move to integrated development. They realized that crop replacement, although supported by the Thai government, was the agenda of international agencies answering drug problems in Europe and North America. As familiarity of hill conditions grew among the Thai, they planned broader methodologies of which crop substitution was a part, that responded more appropriately to local problems and conditions. This approach would also enable the highland work to come under the framework of national economic and social development.

Going into the second decade of highland work, the novelty, and some of the idealism, of the 1970s vanished. The culture of highland development work was being established with certain expectations on the part of both the officials and the hill people. The newness, the excitement of embarking on a grand mission, and the ad hoc inventiveness, faded away in the increasing plans and forms of development work.

INTEGRATED RURAL DEVELOPMENT

The following overviews show how these general multi-sectoral undertakings fit more closely within Thailand's national socioeconomic development policies. During this time, the government began eradicating opium poppy. Even such "difficult" villages such as Pa Kluai agreed to stop opium cultivation.

MAE SA INTEGRATED WATERSHED AND FOREST LAND USE PROJECT

Starting at least with the FAO survey of 1956–1957 showing extensive forest damage, Thai leaders worried over forest depletion. When government attention began turning to hill people and what were perceived to be problems they caused, the Royal Forest Department (RFD) concluded that highlanders were destroying the hills through shifting cultivation.[4] This

---

4. Although the belief that shifting cultivation destroys the forest came from European foresters, recent studies by Western scientists have, for at least three decades, belied this. F. R. Moorman, an FAO expert, concluded in 1967 that, "Contrary to a widespread belief, the shifting cultivation as

integrated watershed development project was designed in response to these concerns and in order to find a way for people, who could not for various reasons be relocated, to make a living in ways the RFD approved. Coincidentally, this project was the sort of initiative Williams described in his 1979 report.

The project's objective was to devise a watershed management model addressing what project documentation called "incorrect land use, insecure land tenure, poor cultivation practices, and inefficient utilization of the resource potential" (FAO 1978, p. 2). Among the objectives were the introduction of "new cropping patterns and cultivation practices, education and health measures, market promotion, and secure land tenure according to the capability and availability of the land" (FAO 1978, p. 5). The major poppy growing area around the Hmong village of Mae Sa Mai was located in the watershed. The original project ran from 1973 until 1978 with a second phase lasting until 1981.

At the end of the first period, an interim report proposed that the hill people be settled down "with all possible speed . . . as permanent farmers." The report also suggested that they be provided with agricultural incentives and that extension activities be implemented (FAO 1978, p. 51). Opium production figures for villages such as Mae Sa Mai are not available but secondary data indicates that no reduction of cultivation occurred during the project's life. No significant progress was made in securing the hill people with citizenship or land

---

practiced by the hilltribes does not lead to any grave soil deterioration . . . soil erosion is rare, and we have as yet not observed any serious accelerated wash-off or gully erosion" (United Nations Survey Team 1967, p. 128; see also Zinke et al., in Kunstadter et al. 1978, pp. 134–159). Nonetheless, the Royal Forest Department has persistently opposed shifting cultivation.

rights although a leasehold arrangement giving land use rights to the people was proposed (FAO 1978, pp. 95–102).

MAE CHAEM INTEGRATED WATERSHED
DEVELOPMENT PROJECT

Also a project to develop a watershed with a major opium-producing site, this U.S.-supported initiative operated from 1980–1987 in a river valley running north to south just west of Chiang Mai.[5] The area was also chosen because of some security problems.[6] The project paper stated that the project would "provide the minimum essential requirements for initiating and sustaining the economic development process in the Watershed" (USAID/Thailand 1980, p. vi). According to annex 1 of the project agreement, the project was designed to "establish a self-sustaining upward trend in real income and access to social services. . . while reversing the deterioration in environmental quality."

Despite Mae Chaem being a major poppy growing region, the project's direct objectives did not include opium replacement. Planners believed that since opium was a poverty indicator and that when development activities raised income, poppy cultivation would decline. It was believed this approach was also more suitable to the many lowland Thais living in the

5. The CRCDP villages of Ban Phui and Mae Tho are either in or just outside of Mae Chaem.

6. A previous district officer was killed by insurgents. Occasional armed conflicts occurred there in the late 1970s and army units patrolled the valley.

project area (Roth et al. 1983, pp. 172–173). The Office of the Permanent Secretary of the Ministry of Agriculture and Cooperatives was the implementing agency.

The Thai government agreed with USAID that land-use certificates should be issued to rural farmers. This would give them legal rights to their land and the confidence to cooperate in development activities and to undertake risky ventures (Kampe 1989, p. 21). When it came time to implement this arrangement, the Royal Forest Department said to do so would violate their regulations. In response USAID withheld funding for about a year starting in February 1982 until the Thai Cabinet decided to exempt this area from RFD's regulations. Eventually over 4,000 permits would be issued. This was the only highland project to obtain such permits for the people in its area.

Serious problems encountered in project management were resolved by first moving the project headquarters from Bangkok to Chiang Mai in 1982 when the provincial governor was made the project manager. To handle routine business, he appointed a well-trusted former district officer from Mae Chaem as deputy director. In 1984, when the project headquarters was moved to Mae Chaem itself, management problems were mainly resolved.

These changes towards increased localization and people's participation paralleled developments in other projects. To enhance local participation, the project hired "interface teams," mostly highly motivated and well-educated young people who would live in the project villages to befriend the people and learn more deeply what their problems were. Another project initiative was to increase the cultivation of subsistence crops such as upland rice by the hill people and the Thais.

THAI-AUSTRALIAN HIGHLAND AGRICULTURAL AND SOCIAL DEVELOPMENT PROJECT

Australian aid for opium replacement and highland development in northern Thailand began in 1971 with a study of upland pastures. Australian aid commenced in 1972 to promote livestock raising to utilize grasslands left after intensive opium cultivation had reduced soil fertility. In 1977, the Australians decided that crop production was more important, and under the name of the Thai-Australian Agricultural Project, worked to develop food crops such as hill rice, corn, and potatoes while also preventing soil erosion (Robert and Renard 1989, p. 27).

Additional Australian assistance followed a request by Thailand to the World Bank to help implement a forest settlement project in the north. The bank favored a wider approach aimed at increasing lowland production and better utilizing highland resources. After the project started in 1979, Australian assistance commenced in 1979 and became the major funding source by 1986 (Hoare 1986, pp. 143–145). Eventually there were three components of Australian-funded work: the Thai-Australian World Bank Land Development Project (TAWLD) working with the Land Development Department; the Highland Agricultural and Social Development Project (HASD) working with the Public Welfare Department; and highland forestry work with the Royal Forest Department (Hoare 1986, p. 144).

HASD worked in 48 key villages and 249 satellite villages in nine zones over five provinces that had not been reached by the other projects. Aside from the Royal Project, HASD was the geographically most diverse of the projects. Its primary goal was "to improve the environmental, social and economic welfare of the hilltribe people of northern Thailand." The primary focus was on agricultural development but HASD also supported building schools and health facilities. Here too, opium reduction was not stated as a primary project goal although there were poppy-growing areas in the sites.

A major undertaking by HASD was to introduce a rotational system of cultivation on fixed plots to replace shifting cultivation, allow food and cash crop production, and not damage the environment. Grass strips planted at regular levels in the fields would separate the plots of individual crops. They were also meant to reduce soil loss on cultivated hillsides (HASD 1987, p. 9). In the mid 1980s, this approach to highland agriculture was viewed widely by developers in northern Thailand as an appropriate answer to shifting cultivation. They believed it offered the chance to grow a diversity of crops annually in the hills in an area less than had been needed for swiddening and in an environmentally sound manner.

THAI-GERMAN HIGHLAND DEVELOPMENT
PROGRAMME (TG-HDP)

The German development agency, GTZ supported a project in Chiang Rai and Mae Hong Son that was to be the lengthiest of all the initiatives. Beginning in 1981 in the Chiang Rai district of Mae Suai (*tambon* Wawi area), the project later expanded to two other areas in Mae Hong Son (Nam Lang and Huai Poo Ling (Huai Phu Ling)) before its completion in 1999. Also working in areas with a diverse population and high poppy cultivation, the goal of TG-HDP was "to devise and implement a strategy to solve, as far as possible, the socio-economic and ecological problems of the three project sites" [in which TG would work] (Brandenberg 1985, p. 5). As such this followed the integrated watershed development approach called for by Williams. The Office of Narcotics Control Board was the implementing agency.

Tambon Wawi was an area of mixed settlement with all the area's highland ethnic groups except the Hmong, as well as Yunnanese Chinese who had come originally to trade in opium. The cosmopolitan village of Wawi traded in opium, tea, and other products.[7] Trafficking routes linked Wawi with important opium-growing areas such as Doi Chang in the south of the project area with border sites like the Akha village of Pha Mi, and those inside Myanmar.

Instead of creating a specific project to be implemented, project planners opted for a "program" by which flexibility would be stressed and adjustments could be readily accomplished. This would enable the program to respond to conditions in the project sites with which the project staff was unfamiliar. To ensure good relations with the people, contact teams similar to the interface teams in the Mae Chaem Project were established to bridge gaps between highlanders and project personnel. Since it took over two years for these teams to be organized, involvement of the *tambon* Wawi villagers was initially limited (BMZ and GTZ 1983, p. 41). In 1986, the next evaluation of the program suggested that "Special training sessions must be organized in order to make the concepts of people participation and self reliance known among the Project personnel" (including the contact team members who were now on the job) (Chayan 1986, p. 3).

Environmental concerns arose. The use of the grass strips pioneered by HASD in *tambon* Wawi met with problems.

---

7. Tea as traditionally used in the neighboring countries of northern Thailand was fermented and chewed. Known as *miang*, it was the most lucrative highland trade item in the north prior to the cash cropping of opium.

Despite vigorous efforts to find grasses that would not escape the strips, the effort ended without success. At present this once widely heralded cropping system is hardly used, if at all.

Just as the Hmong had developed cabbage cultivation, hill people here found a lucrative market for tomato for a couple of years. Unlike the cabbage, the market was short-lived (and the problem of pests greater than with cabbage) so that tomato is grown only in moderate amounts in *tambon* Wawi.

Because, as elsewhere, the cash crops identified yielded less cash per area than opium, the villagers cleared forest land to make way for new cultivation sites. As mortality declined in the hills and migrants from outside the area entered the project sites, the population increased. Even more pressure was put on the forests, resulting in considerable depletion in some areas.

THAI-NORWEGIAN CHURCH AID HIGHLAND DEVELOPMENT PROJECT (TN-HDP)

Reflecting the United Nation's efforts to attract donors, Norwegian Church Aid agreed to operate this project under the UN umbrella while maintaining its own name. Norwegian Church Aid, run under the national church of Norway, raised funds in a variety of ways including mass campaigns to make the project visible to its donors.

Starting after the completion of HAMP in 1984, this project followed the general integrated development approach. Because the project operated in areas with a large Karen population, which grew little poppy, the main objective was to increase the efficiency of subsistence farming. Replacing the opium poppy and improving health, sanitation and other services were secondary objectives. A new objective, perhaps in response to comments such as those by Paul Lewis that

TG-HDP

Clean drinking water

projects lacked the participation of the people, the fourth objective was to "encourage and support local initiative projects for self-development. . . ."[8] Three project sites were selected. Two were in Chiang Mai province inhabited mainly by Karen but also with a few Hmong villages such as the HAMP village of Pa Kluai, and the third at the convergence of Lampang and Phayao provinces where Yao and Lisu were settled and another old HAMP village was located. The

8. Problem censuses were administered in all project villages with help from the Tribal Research Institute.

project's counterpart was the Public Welfare Department. The original project life was from 1985 until 1989; an extension for certain activities continued until 1991.

OTHER UNITED NATIONS PROJECTS

In 1986 and 1987, three new United Nations projects were started. These were the Pae Por, Sam Mun, and Wiang Pha Highland Development Projects. All three operated in areas of Chiang Mai province not yet covered by existing projects. The Pae Por Project, covering an area populated almost entirely by Karen, also included the northern portion of Tak province. Although executed by different counterpart agencies (Pae Por by the Department of Local Administration, and Sam Mun and Wiang Pha by the Royal Forest Department, the basic approach of the three was similar.

All were integrated highland development projects conducted in and around areas with opium cultivation. The development objectives in Sam Mun and Wiang Pha project documents are identical beginning with the same statement: "The project aims at improving the quality of life among the hilltribes through the implementation of an integrated rural development project."[9] Supporting the government policy to eliminate cultivation and addiction to opium are mentioned secondarily. The project documents refer to ending poppy cultivation only as the second immediate objective for agriculture, after increasing food production and food self-sufficiency

---

9. Only one word is different. Sam Mun states: "opium poppy and addiction to its products"; Wiang Pha states: "opium poppy and addiction to its derivatives".

(Thai-UN Sam Mun HDP 1987, pp. 1, 3; Thai-UN Wiang Pha HDP, pp. 1,3).

THE THAI THIRD ARMY

The Third Army implemented a project starting in 1983 together with ONCB in the Doi Yao and Doi Pha Mon area on the Lao border in the east of Chiang Rai province. The army took the lead in this project because it was a high security zone where highland insurgency persisted longer than elsewhere in the north. Perhaps because the army played a leading role and was concerned over the income the insurgents might gain from the poppy, the project's objective was to "terminate opium poppy cultivation." Secondary objectives were "to improve the standard of living of the hilltribesmen through community development and crop replacement programmes." From 49 target villages in 1983, the project expanded its scope to 136 by 1987 (Yingyos 1987, p. 88). It would not be until the end of the decade that the UN took over the implementation of the project.

DRUG CONTROL

The leadership of most of these projects came from fields such as agriculture, community government, the military, and forestry. ONCB was still in its formative stages and for the Thai government, drug control at this time still meant law enforcement. Little emphasis was placed on drug demand reduction. Norwegian Church Aid began in 1988 to support a project to reduce opium addiction by hill people in Kamphaeng Phet. Besides this, little demand reduction work was carried out in the hills. The 1988 *Thailand Narcotics Annual Report* makes

Karen weaving on backstrap loom

no specific reference to drug prevention or education in the hills (ONCB 1988).

As the projects were designed, attention still lay on crop replacement and aspects of society related to marketing, such as new roads. The new projects being designed paid little attention to drug control. To cite but one example, the 1991 terminal evaluation of the Pae Por Highland Development Project noted high rates of drug addiction and high recidivism following drug detoxification (Francis et al. 1991, pp. 44–45). No serious mention is made in either the project document or the terminal evaluation of preventive education or demand reduction.

What the report does mention is a project supported by the United States to eradicate opium poppy. Although the government began surveying poppy fields in 1979, eradication did not commence until 1984 and then only in areas where it was thought the people could make a satisfactory living without relying on opium.

Little attention was being paid to treating drug addiction or providing information on new substances. Opium poppy was beginning to be cut down in villages where more income was being earned. Influence from the outside was entering the hills on newly built roads and through schools and non-formal educational programs then being set up. Hill people were going to town more, to shop, to sightsee, and to go to school. The economy of the country was growing rapidly, producing various impacts on the hills and the people. These changing factors would be played out in the coming years with sometimes unexpected consequences.

RECENT PARTICIPATORY ALTERNATIVE DEVELOPMENT APPROACHES

In about 1980, developers throughout the world concluded that they needed to involve the people more in their work. In a process taking over a decade, some of the most prominent thinkers on development theory, such as Robert Chambers, concluded that many past errors arose from the domination of the development process by those in power. By analyzing mistakes in previous development projects, Chambers and his associates devised a process known as PRA (Participatory Rural Appraisal) that amounts to a methodological revolution. Chambers concluded that rural people, often illiterate, are remarkably capable of expressing their local realities even when they exhibit great complexity (Chambers 1997). The popularity of this school of thought has been astonishing, influencing development projects throughout the world.

But perhaps Chambers was not the first participatory developer. His Majesty King Bhumibol Adulyadej pioneered participatory highland initiatives as early as 1972 when he suggested that Huai Hong Khrai, in Doi Saket to the east of Chiang Mai, be the site of a Development Study Center to find ways for developing degraded watershed source forests. At these and other such study centers around the country, the king brought together government officials from different agencies to exchange ideas with the people in order to improve the people's lives.

In the early 1980s, His Majesty spoke often of the need to involve the people in development. In calling for improving villager self-sufficiency, he explained that by enabling them to grow food crops they could improve their standard of living in what he called an "explosion from within." In an address to Chulalongkorn University students in 1980, the king advised, "you should above all work slowly and cautiously. . . . Do not hurry out of a hunger to build something new for the sake of novelty. There is in fact nothing really new. Everything new arises out of the old and will itself become old later on." In this spirit, he noted that "Advising is not ordering but presenting the theory of the activity for people to hear and to consider. If they like it they will do it; but if not then never mind" (RDPB 1997, p. 256, 253).

These ideas appealed to the Thai generation of the 1970s that was influenced by student activism in Europe and North America. This decade in Thailand was marked by two major uprisings that shaped the youth of the time. One culminated on 14 October 1973 with the removal of three unpopular military leaders who left the country. The second ended on 6

October 1976 with the return of the armed forces to power. In subsequent years, the youth of the 1970s began to work for more democracy and greater openness in government.[10]

Members of this generation worked not only in projects such as the CRCDP. Other Thai youth established new organizations including NGOs that worked in many sectors of society to build a civil society. Many in this generation saw work in NGOs as a way to work from the bottom up to bring about a better way of life for rural people. Within the government, new programs were created as old ones were reformed.

HILL AREAS EDUCATION PROGRAM

Besides the king's early participatory work, the Hill Areas Education Program of the Non-formal Education Department was another such initiative before the development world "invented" the concept. Arising out of a Public Welfare and Adult Education Division, later the Non-formal Education Department Effort to Promote Thai Literacy, this USAID-funded project began operations in 1980 and furthered an educational initiative entitled *khit pen* (being able to think) pioneered by Kowit Woraphiphat.[11] Together with Ekawit Nathalang, then a deputy director general in the ministry, Kowit devised an educational program for hill people.

---

10. A large number of youth, perhaps 2,000–3,000, left the cities to join uprisings in the hills, sometimes in areas where development projects were operating. By 1980, almost all had returned to the mainstream.

11. U.S. policy at the time dictated that hill area projects had to have opium control as a principal objective even it were not stated in the project paper.

According to the project paper, its purpose was "to develop and test, through inter-agency involvement, in six sites and approximately 36 villages a community-based and replicable non-formal basic education model more appropriate to the needs and conditions existing in remote hill areas than presently available education. This model will make extensive use of village level resources and participation in all phases of model development" (USAID 1980 p. 9; Kampe, interview).

The model developed called for establishing educational centers (known as *ashram*, taken from the Pali-Sanskrit word meaning a retreat for the instruction of holy people) which would serve a cluster of villages. Qualifications for teachers required such attributes as "devotion to duty" and "sense of responsibility" rather than academic degrees or years of experience. The teachers were to encourage learning that would have such practical goals as obtaining Thai citizenship for the villagers, providing preventive drug education to counter new drug use patterns, or eradicating crop pests. With the participation of the community the *ashram* was designed to use any means to achieve these goals. HAEP was, in fact, "a nonformal model for education and development" (HAEP 1986, p. 92). The curriculum was non-graded and not dependent on the time spent studying. Basically, when a student had learned enough to complete the six year basic education curriculum he or she could do so. Later Princess Maha Chakri gave these *ashrams* a royal title—*Sunkansuksa Mae Fa Luang*, The Princess Mother's Educational Centers.

Although the program, in the end, was gradually institutionalized by requiring that the teachers held academic degrees making the learning like conventional (formal) education, HAEP helped train a large number of individuals working in the hills. This included teachers, Thai officials in the Non-formal Education Department, the hill people themselves, and persons in various pursuits from the UN to Parliament. They started projects, NGOs, foundations, and new initiatives within the government that had a significant overall impact on highland development work.

MORE PARTICIPATORY WORK

The transition to more participatory work occurred at about the same time and because of some of the same factors as the Declaration of the International Conference on Drug Abuse in 1987. This was made at a conference in Vienna attended by representatives of 138 states and 200 non-governmental organizations. This declaration, which mandated "universal action to combat the drug problem in all its forms" (United Nations Division of Narcotic Drugs 1988, p. iii) encouraged widening the scope of the fight against drugs. The declaration recognized drug demand reduction as a necessary tool in countering drug use.

This widened the scope of highland development. In the 1970s, the approach was in principal law enforcement. Because the enforcers recognized they would not succeed, they created an improvisational approach that blended community development and suppression. This constituted only one-third of what the UN now defines as alternative development. Moving into the 1980s, the scope would widen further.

ONCB recognized the need for conducting more demand reduction work and involving local communities in its efforts. The seemingly unstoppable increase of heroin use in the hills demanded new approaches. A few years would pass, though, until 1994 when ONCB initiated a study entitled "Model for Solutions to Drug Problems at the Field Level Focusing on Community Roles and Government and NGO Mechanisms

Facilitating Problem Solution in the Community" in 150 villages in the country's four regions. The study found that to make the best use of local potential, a flexible multifold response was needed in which officials should be supportive rather than directive. In 1997, the Cabinet authorized ONCB to use Community-Based Drug Abuse Control in 1,145 villages identified as having severe drug problems (CB-DAC Core Team 1997, p. ii).

New directions were also taken by the highland development projects. When for example the Mae Chaem project was concluded in 1989, much of the work was taken over by Care International with an emphasis on activities in community forestry and drug treatment, particularly for heroin users. The trend for more participatory work was also reflected in the United Nations development projects of the time.

THAI-UN PROJECTS

Following the increased availability of heroin in northern Thailand, many highland development projects, even those without an emphasis on drug control, reassessed their policies regarding drugs. During the early 1990s, several projects showed a fresh interest in drug control, particularly demand reduction.

More community-based work of all types was initiated, in particular in drug treatment during the latter phases of some projects. During a one-and-a-half-year extension of the Sam Mun Project one main objective was to develop and strengthen the capacity of community organizations to conduct development activities as well as drug treatment and rehabilitation. Two forestry officials in the Sam Mun Project, Pakorn Jingsoongnern and Samer Limchoowong, helped formulate participatory land use processes that became models for other projects. The main objectives for the final extension of the Thai-Norway Project, from 1993–1995, were to use community approaches to reduce the number of addicts and increase women's participation in development (Chaiwat 1994, pp. 8–9).

In many villages, new social organizations were established. These included women's groups, youth groups, vocational groups that worked to produce and market village handicrafts, as well as credit and revolving fund groups. The projects spent considerable effort on creating these new organizations as a means of strengthening local capacity and initiative.

A newly designed project, the Integrated Pockets Area Development Project (IPAD) was established from 1991–1994 in poppy-growing regions so small or isolated that they had been overlooked in the previous work. In eradicating drug production, the project emphasized developing social groups, leaders, and citizen participation.

UNITED NATIONS SUPPORTED DEMAND REDUCTION WORK IN THE HILLS

In the mid 1990s, UN support was provided to the Integrated Drug Abuse Prevention Project (IDAP) in Chiang Mai and Mae Hong Son, the Strengthening of Community-based Drug Prevention Strategies in the Highlands of Northern Thailand, and the Development of Drug Dependence Treatment for Hilltribe Communities Project. Other demand reduction work was carried out in a Myanmar border area project. ONCB also cooperated in hosting, together with the National Welfare Council of Thailand and UNDCP, the 1994 NGO World Forum on Drug Demand Reduction. Such projects demonstrate official acceptance of participatory work, the need for demand reduction, and the increased role of NGOs.

THAI-GERMAN HIGHLAND DEVELOPMENT PROGRAMME

By the end of its life, in 1998, TG-HDP had changed its focus to involve the villagers in most areas of its work. The program was working to strengthen people's organizations such as credit groups, rice banks, and the *tambon* administrative council, with the hope that these people's organizations would make the work that the project had introduced sustainable. While the UN projects discussed above had already begun implementing these activities, it is in TG-HDP that they are seen the most clearly.

In a tone far different from that in the evaluations of the 1980s, TG-HDP admitted in 1998 that:

All too often we in TG-HDP have heard villagers complain that "all you ever do is conduct surveys; we are sick of it." All too often, also, we developers have complained about the lack of cooperation by the people. But in fact this lack of cooperation is not caused by just the villagers. It also comes from the developers' attitudes and the techniques we use (Naret et al. 1998, p. 21).

From 1994–1998, the Thai-German Programme had carried out four special projects in its Huai Phu Ling area in Mae Hong Son province: community-based (environmentally friendly) land use planning, community-based drug abuse control, off-farm activities, and rural financial management. Activities began with community research by the villagers to draw up a village development plan.

As with several UN projects, TG-HDP recognized the

growing problem of drug use. Following a survey of drug use in their Mae Hong Son sites, TG-HDP leaders grew so worried over heroin, that they made its control a focus for programme work (CB-DAC Core Team 1997, p. 17). Rather than relying on institutional treatment, and in line with the programme's shift to participatory work, community-based drug control was begun. TG-HDP realized that the awareness and the impetus for "attacking the problem must come from the community itself, with initial facilitation by government and project staff" (CB-DAC Core Team 1997, p. viii). The community was involved at all levels of drug prevention and control, with the community accepting that drugs were its own problem. In this work, drug control was integrated with activities in other sectors. In the first year of concerted work, the number of users in the project areas declined from 511 in 1993 to 271 in 1994. Continued progress was made in later years (CB-DAC Core Team 1997). Positive results were recorded in many other villages. One case is as follows.

CASE STUDY OF A LAHU VILLAGE

Some villages, such as the Black Lahu village of Ja Bo in the Huai Phu Ling Area, managed to eliminate opium. When TG-HDP began work, the people's organizations believed resource management and agricultural were more important. But when encouraged by the TG-HDP staff to draw up the village plan, the villagers carefully reviewed the issue of drug use in Ja Bo. Once they decided that they could indeed eliminate drugs, they collected information on user families to determine the resolve of the addicts. Village leaders then planned a four-month treatment course with the TG-HDP staff. The role of the latter was reduced mainly due to introducing rehabilitation and vocational training expert to the villagers. These experts served as the trainers in the rehabilitation process but turned over the work to the villagers in the monitoring phase (Chatchai 1998, pp. 65–66).

A SUMMARY

The projects in the 1990s took place amidst an increasingly active Thai government program in the hills. The growing economy enabled the government to implement the highland master plans. New schools and health facilities were set up in hundreds of villages. Thousands of kilometers of roads linked places previously separated from lowland market centers by several days' walk. Electrification and communications facilities brought once isolated villages into national life and even the Internet. Tourism into the hills and migration to the cities created new links between peoples that had rarely encountered one another.

Certain neighborhoods in Chiang Mai and various types of jobs, generally low-paying and in service sectors, came to be dominated by hill people. Highland women became involved in prostitution, and HIV/AIDS was transferred to the hill people. Hill area migrants from Myanmar or Laos came to Thailand. The population mobility contributed to a resurgence of malaria and other communicable diseases.

New environmental concerns were raised. Following the roads into the hills, private entrepreneurs built resorts—some very close to old HAMP villages such as Mae Sa Mai—as well as golf courses, residences, and commercial agricultural undertakings. Although these problems mainly lay outside the scope of opium replacement, the projects helped the people protect themselves through better awareness.

As changes took place in the hills, the primacy of highland projects in affecting highland life declined. Whereas in the 1970s, when the money from the projects was unprecedented, by the 1990s, its financial impact was significantly less. Assessing the total impact of the highland projects during this time grows more problematic.

The significance of the highland projects in the 1990s was their introduction of new ideas and methods of working. Participatory planning and the work to create learning organizations within the communities proved to be more effective ways for dealing with drug problems than anything done previously.

A BALANCED APPROACH: ALTERNATIVE DEVELOPMENT, DEMAND REDUCTION, AND LAW ENFORCEMENT

As projects were learning through experience the ways of the hills and how to work there, a groundswell of dissatisfaction with highland development arose. Besides the former concerns over the issues of citizenship and forest use, and the dissatisfaction over project implementation in the unfamiliar highland context, new complaints came up related to projects and their impact, and to conditions beyond the ambit of highland development work per se. Projects were criticized for:

- making conditions so difficult for opium to be grown within Thailand that the cultivators moved to Myanmar where the opium they grew was processed into heroin and then smuggled back into Thailand.
- spending too much on experts, infrastructure, and activities that were unsuccessful.
- forcing the hill people out of many of their old locales to make way for national parks, forest reserves, and resorts.
- not actually reducing opium until poppy suppression was implemented.
- stripping the people of their culture and turning them into imitations of modern lowland Thai.
- contributing to the spread of heroin in the hills.

There is truth in these arguments. But they overlook much. Reviewing the entire Thai journey through three decades of opium poppy replacement and highland development, one should regard it primarily as a learning experience.[1] At the start of the process, in the 1960s, no one in the Thai government knew about the hilltribes or poppy cultivation. There was only one trained anthropologist in Thailand and he was busy teaching in Bangkok. No one in the government spoke hilltribe languages. Roads barely reached the base of the hills and the hill people rarely came to town. There were hardly any schools in the hills and, among the opium growing groups, only some men had learned some northern Thai from visiting the market towns. Probably no hilltribe person had earned a Thai college degree before 1960. Only a few Westerners (i.e. Bernatzik 1947) had studied opium growing groups before the 1950s. When in 1958 Geddes entered the Hmong village for his anthropological study at Mae Tho in Chiang Mai, he was met with indifference and a lack of cooperation, the villagers thinking he had come to buy or beg opium (Geddes 1976, p. v).

Little was known about replacement crops. Chiang Mai University was established in 1964 and it would be years before it had sufficient expertise in food science and agriculture to help the highland projects. There was no marketing infrastructure, no roads, and no personal contacts for marketing anything from the hills except opium, forest produce, and fermented tea *(miang)*. There were no proven highland cropping or agro-forestry schemes that could be readily introduced for use.

---

1. For most of this period, UNDCP guidelines on alternative development had not been devised; as much as any organization the UN learned from the Thai experience.

The country's educational system had, besides teaching people to be Thai, taught students implicitly that non-Thais did not belong to Thailand. Generations of officials believed that Thai people were Buddhist, spoke Thai, grew lowland rice, enjoyed a long shared history originating in the south of China, and participated in various Thai festivals. Hilltribes looked nothing like Thais to most officials. While Chinese in cities had somehow become Thai, many of them still appeared somewhat different to the average Thai. Hilltribes, however, looked completely alien to the average Thai.

At the international level, there were other misconceptions. No less a figure than Giuseppe di Gennaro, UNFDAC executive director in the early 1980s recognized this. As he wrote himself, in a meeting he had with King Bhumibol Adulyadej on 30 June 1982,

> The King said that—according to his point of view—at least thirty years would be required to complete the task.
>
> I ... [pointed] out that thirty years was an unacceptable time frame. No serious planning could be so long term. Within such a time span, so many independent variables could hinder the productivity of any investment.
>
> I tried to let His Majesty understand that if I proposed such a long time frame to my donors, they would disappear. The King listened in silence. I was sure I had changed His Majesty's mind. But when, after the audience, I mentioned this feeling to those accompanying me, they explained that it is a Thai custom not to react in such circumstances. Silence did not mean acceptance" [di Gennaro 1991, p. 60).

IN RESPONSE: EVOLUTION OF THE THAI BALANCED APPROACH

The Thai government, however, in the pragmatic way that has characterized its political survival for centuries,[2] addressed the problem forthrightly. In cooperation with international agencies, in particular the United Nations drug control agencies, studies were conducted in the 1960s. Together with help from the Colombo Plan, the Tribal Research Centre (later Institute) was set up in 1964, under which mainly Australian and New Zealand scholars were brought to help study the hill people and train Thai officials. By the 1970s an increasing body of knowledge and Thai expertise existed on the hill people and their cultures. Work continued through HAEP programs and other initiatives.

The early initiatives, despite their problems in getting to know the hill people and elicit their participation in development work before the Thai knew much about the hill people, still managed to identify numerous potential sources of income from cash crops to handicrafts to agro-forestry. These initiatives explored marketing possibilities and established links with major food processing companies in Thailand. Infrastructure development facilitated the marketing of some goods. Advice from His Majesty forestalled poppy destruction until suitable alternatives became available.

2. Two examples include Thailand's survival in World War II and the effort to reduce fertility in the 1960s and 1970s. In the former, despite cooperating with the Japanese during the war and allowing Japanese troops access to the country, a change in prime ministers in 1944 and a friendship with the U.S. on whom Thailand had not declared war, enabled the country to make peace with Great Britain and France and join the UN in 1947. In the latter, following a creative campaign, Thailand was recognized by the UNFPA (now, the United Nations Population Fund) and others as a success in reducing fertility in the 1970s.

During the integrated rural development projects of the 1980s, more efforts to bring the hill people within the Thai polity began. Thai government services in health and education entered the hills. Serious efforts to grant hill people Thai citizenship were begun simultaneously with poppy destruction. The government sent the message from 1984 on to the hill people that citizenship could be offered to those abandoning poppy cultivation. Although implementing this proved difficult, from then on, more hill people obtained citizenship and sent their children to Thai schools. The size of the projects and the involvement of many agencies acquainted a large number of Thai officials with the hill people. Although misconceptions about them persisted in the big cities, people on the ground began to know hill people better than ever before.

In the era of participatory projects in the 1990s, Thai officials and a growing number of NGOs in the hills began to trust the hill people sufficiently to involve them fully in project planning and implementation. Thai officials realized too that involving the hill people was also necessary for effective work. In this regard, the much-debated Community Forestry Bill was nearing approval (although the outcome remains in doubt at the writing of this report). Hill people entered the government service, earned college degrees, and many became teachers in the hills. By the 1990s only a small amount of opium cultivation persisted, encouraged by the high price it commanded because of its scarcity.

The absence of a Thai highland authority and the ending of all the UN and bilateral highland projects had the unintended result that the lessons of the overall experience were never written down. Much has been lost as reports go missing and people involved in the work move on to new agencies or retire from government service. Only among some UN staff and consultants as well as in the NGOs has the body of knowledge on the Thai hill people persisted. However, because they are so diverse and generally small, the successes of the Thai balanced approach have never been formally collected.

Thailand's balanced approach combines the following components:

1. Alternative Development with People's Participation

Thailand's work included campaigning against opium use, promoting socioeconomic development, and the participation of the people. Different agencies, including NGOs and private enterprises, as they became active in hill work, began to carry out various aspects of these three components. The various income-generating activities and the infrastructure established made it possible for the opium growers to make a living without the poppy.

2. Demand Reduction

Thailand began conducting an active demand reduction program during the 1980s. In hill areas, and with help from NGOs, Thai as well as hilltribe language media have been used. ONCB works with the Ministry of Education in school-based programs and with *tambon* councils and other people's organizations as well as NGOs in various drug prevention initiatives. With opium, the work has been quite effective; with heroin, progress has been made but the substance's addictiveness has impeded results.

3. Law Enforcement

Starting in 1984, ONCB began cooperating with the Border Patrol Police and the army to engage in a poppy destruction program. The coordinated use of satellite imagery, aerial surveys, and ground inspection are now used to control the cultivation of poppies in the face of the increasing ingenuity of cultivators in evading detection.

4. Ample and Long-term Investment

International donors began investing in crop replacement in Thailand in the 1970s. Since then, NGOs, the private sector, and the government have invested hundreds of millions of dollars as well as an inestimable amount of volunteer time in opium replacement and highland development. Of the large amounts provided by international donors and NGOs, a greater proportion has been used to develop opium areas than non-opium areas. By contrast, the government's investment has been spread throughout the hills more evenly.

5. National Unity

Under the moral leadership of King Bhumibol Adulyadej, Thailand identified opium poppy replacement as a national priority. Without this, the heavy investment in government and private funds could not have taken place. Through frequent visits to hill areas starting in the late 1960s, the king inspired loyalty to Thailand among the hill people and made them more willing to participate in the alternative development work. As he visited the hill people, the government provided increasing amounts of funding to build roads and carry out other infrastructure improvements in those places. Besides enhancing the development process, law enforcement efforts became more effective.

LEADERSHIP IN ALTERNATIVE
DEVELOPMENT EFFORTS

Leadership in alternative development work has come from many sources and at various levels. The royal family, government agencies and NGOs, and international donors have lent leadership in different ways to opium replacement initiatives.

The royal family provided moral authority to replacing opium which supported national unity. The king's creativity, concern for the common people, and influence over the government provided informal guidelines for opium replacement that were holistic, humane, and progressive.

The government brought crop replacement into the general development work of the country. To overcome overlapping departmental authority, inappropriate rules and regulations, as well as vested interests, the government drafted highland master plans that sought to give all the work a single focus. When the Thai economy boomed, the government was able to allocate budgets sufficiently large to bring more services into the hills to benefit the residents.

NGOs provided leadership that worked mainly at the grass-roots level. They worked to strengthen people's organizations and represented the hill people in dealing with the government. Some ways for dealing with hill problems pioneered by NGOs have "trickled up" and been adopted by the government.

International donors have supported the entire process. Without foreign funding, the opium replacement process would have started much later and proceeded more slowly. After 1990, when development work entered a more participatory phase, leadership provided by international donors has often merged with that of the NGOs and, to a certain extent, with that provided by the government.

ROYALLY SPONSORED PROJECTS

Different members of the royal family for over a century have taken an interest in the hill people of the kingdom. One of the titles adopted by King Mongkut (Rama IV) in the mid nineteenth century was "King of the Karens." King Chulalongkorn (Rama V) visited the Karens in Kanchanaburi several times. His successors, King Vajiravudh and Prajadhipok (Rama VI and VII) visited Chiang Mai and met many tribal groups. But it has been the present royal family which has taken the greatest interest, devoting considerable time, funds, and creativity.

KING BHUMIBOL ADULYADEJ AND THE ROYAL PROJECT

The work of the Royal Project, which developed from the king's work and that of the Royal Assistance Unit, has realized his vision, aided by his ability to facilitate cooperation between agencies. He used his own funds and was helped by the voluntary work of his staff and government officials. He also received contributions from charitable organizations, commercial firms, and many individuals, rich and poor, as well as foreign governments and international agencies.

No formal evaluation has ever been undertaken, but the total investment is well over US$150 million. Because of the many in-kind contributions by official agencies and interested individuals, the exact total is inestimable.

The Royal Project at present operates in about three hundred villages in Chiang Mai, Chiang Rai, Lamphun, Mae Hong Son, and Phayao provinces. Four research stations and thirty-five development centers support the work. The Royal Project has developed an active marketing component to its work involving post-harvest treatment, transportation, grading and packing, food processing, and market research. For marketing its produce, the most lucrative of which are vegetables, cut flowers, and fruit, the Royal Project has registered the trade name, Doi Kham (Golden Mountains) which it began using in the mid 1980s (*Munlanithi Khrongkan Luang* pp. 29–30). Royal Project produce is sold through its own outlets at airports and shopping centers in the country's major urban centers as well as its own development centers.

The king and the Royal Project arranged for the villagers to grow their crops in their own villages, thus promoting crops that are of use to them in their daily life. The experience has been that vegetables are the most beneficial for the villagers (Suthat interview 2000).

THE PRINCESS MOTHER AND DOI TUNG

Others in the royal family, in particular the Princess Mother, have also taken an interest in highland people. Her earliest efforts helped to establish schools for hilltribes and others living in remote areas. By 1955, she had provided funds to the Border Patrol Police school program based at their headquarters in Camp Dara Ratsami in Chiang Mai. This program to provide primary education in areas unreached by the Ministry of Education opened its first school in 1956 at Don Mahawan village, Chiang Khong district, in Chiang Rai province.

In 1989, UNESCO granted an award to the Border Patrol Police schools for the promotion of literacy. The Princess Mother also took an interest in health problems by establishing the Princess Mother's Volunteer Doctors in 1969 to work in highland and other rural areas.

Her biggest undertaking was to be the Doi Tung Highland Development Project. Doi Tung is a mountain of 1,364 meters in Chiang Rai province, about five kilometers south of the Myanmar border. Located close to transportation routes into Shan State, much traffic, legal and illegal, has passed over and around this mountain for centuries. The Akha and Lahu living there also cultivated considerable amounts of opium. The trade of the poppy flourished in this region, which happened to lie just northwest of Khun Sa's headquarters (until 1982) at Ban Hin Teak on Doi Mae Salong.

The Princess Mother learned of Doi Tung while looking for a site to build an upland palace. Then in her mid eighties, she wanted a place in Thailand with a mild climate where she could stay instead of Lausanne, Switzerland where she had resided much of her life since 1933. When the Princess Mother visited Doi Tung in 1987 she was startled to see the deforestation that had occurred since her first trip there in 1966. She felt the need to rehabilitate the area and help the people (Kanitha, ed. 1998, pp. 91–94).

The Doi Tung Development Project was approved by the Thai Cabinet in 1988. The project comprised work in five sectors: infrastructure, forestry, agriculture, improving the quality of life, and administration. An estimate made in 2000 for the total investment in the Doi Tung Project was 1 billion baht (approx. U.S.$ 25 million).

Unlike the Royal Project, much of its produce is grown under plantation-like conditions. Coffee and macadamia nut are grow in central plots where the local villagers are employed as the working staff and, increasingly, in higher positions.

The royal family's leadership has been far-reaching. Their results have set positive examples for both villagers and government organizations. His Majesty promoted cooperative work between different agencies and with the people while also joining with internationally funded and bilateral activities.

Pha Mi, a village located just northwest of Doi Tung, was subject to the comprehensive attention provided all villages on Doi Tung. All the drug users were treated and told that any relapse would cause them to be moved outside the project. By 1989 a road reached Pha Mi from Doi Tung, one that was subsequently extended northeast to Mae Sai. Village committees were formed, a day care center established, a training center built, and agricultural extension services provided. With no drug use (to speak of) in the village, ready access provided by roads and later telephones, as well as the armed presence of Border Patrol Police and the Thai army, Pha Mi ceased to play a role in the drug trade.

Royal leadership, in an appeal to and influence over all sectors of Thai society, enabled the different stakeholders in the highland development process to move forward together.

GOVERNMENT AND NON-GOVERNMENTAL PROJECTS

The government provided considerable support for highland development, especially from the 1980s when the Thai economy started growing rapidly. In some cases, the government provided facilities in project areas as a part of the counterpart contribution. In other cases, inputs were provided for security reasons or as a part of general national development. Major government support was provided in road building, highland agriculture, and schools.

ROAD BUILDING

Different agencies are responsible for building roads in Thailand. The Department of Highways, Ministry of Transport and Communications, is responsible for highways and roads connecting provincial and district centers. The Department of Accelerated Rural Development, Ministry of Interior, builds roads in rural areas connecting villages with districts and with other villages. The Public Works Department, also in the Ministry of Interior, builds roads in urban areas such as places designated as municipalities or sanitary districts. Military units under the Ministry of Defense build strategic roads in sensitive areas. Before the government established a logging ban in 1989, the Royal Forest Department sometimes built roads. Sometimes also, villagers build unpaved roads using their own labor and other resources.

No one office keeps statistics on road building. However, the highway department headquarters in Chiang Mai province estimates that whereas in 1970 there were almost no roads in the hills, except those for motorcycle use, by 1987 there were approximately 400 kilometers of roads in the hills. Although it is government policy that all roads be paved, at that time only 20 to 30 percent were paved. The construction of these roads was partly a result of the king's visits. Although King Bhumibol Adulyadej usually travels in the hills by helicopter, Thai protocol dictates that whenever he reaches his destination, local officials, from the provincial governor on down, be there to meet him. Many roads were built by various agencies to allow these officials to travel in the hill by motor vehicle to hill villages where the king would be visiting. Because of a desire to support royal activities, when the highway department or other agencies requested funding to build roads to these villages, the Bureau of the Budget responded to these requests (Banlu 2000).

In 2000, it was estimated that highland roads in four northern provinces were as follows:

Chiang Mai: 400 kilometers (80 percent paved)
Mae Hong Son: 300 kilometers (60–70 percent paved)
Lamphun: 150 kilometers (50 percent paved)
Lampang: 100 kilometers (50–60 percent paved)

Construction costs for building highland roads is as follows:

Paved road: 700,000–1,500,000 baht per kilometer
Lateritic roads, Grade A: 4–500,000 baht per kilometer
Grade B: 2–300,000 baht per kilometer

The following table provides some idea of the investment made by the Thai government in paved road building in the

Table 8
ESTIMATED COST OF PAVED ROAD CONSTRUCTION IN THE HILLS

PROVINCE (by kilometer)	PAVED ROAD (in 2001)	AVERAGE COST (Baht)	TOTAL ESTIMATE (Baht)
Chiang Mai	320	1,000,000	320,000,000
Mae Hong Son	180	1,000,000	180,000,000
Lamphun	75	1,000,000	75,000,000
Lampang	55	1,000,000	55,000,000
Total 4 Provinces	620	1,000,000	620,000,000

(1)

(2)

(3)

(4)

The process of bridge building near Som Poi Karen village,
Chom Thong, Chiang Mai

hills. Adding the cost of lateritic roads and unpaved tracks, the total amount invested would have been significantly higher than the approximately 620 million baht (US$15 million in 2000) for paved roads in these four provinces, and then higher again when considering Phayao, Phrae, Nan, and other provinces.

HIGHLAND AGRICULTURE

When highland development work commenced, the Thai government followed the lead of internationally funded projects. The Horticultural Crop Promotion Division as well as agricultural faculties at Kasetsart and Chiang Mai Universities and the Mae Jo Institute for Agricultural Technology (later, university) all contributed to this work. However as donor support declined, the Thai government began to invest more in developing hill area agriculture. From a total budget of 5.2 million baht in 1989 (US$208,000), Thai government funding to the Horticultural Crop Promotion Division alone rose to 61 million baht (US$2,440,000) by 1995. As a part of this, the division oversees eighteen Highland Agriculture Extension Centres in eight provinces, mainly in northwestern Thailand (Horticultural Crop Promotion Division 1996, p. 29, 33).

COMMUNITY SERVICES

Besides the above-mentioned support for highland development, the government also funded schools, health clinics, *tambon* area councils, and other local government units. The totals are difficult to calculate but run to several million dol-

lars per year. When funding to the *tambon* organizations com-
mences, the government funding of hill work will increase substantially.

NON-GOVERNMENTAL ORGANIZATION PROJECTS

Hundreds of NGOs have become active in Thailand, mainly
since the mid 1980s when idealistic youth began seeking new
outlets for their energy. Identifying these groups and deter-
mining their support for highland development is complicated
by the diversity of the groups, the fact that not all sponsor hill
work exclusively, and the desire by some of the groups to
remain unidentified. In the late 1980s when a large number of
NGOs began to work in the hills, different organizations
became interested in the NGO role.

Some government agencies viewed NGOs as potentially
threatening. The Third Army's COHAN surveyed NGOs and
identified approximately twenty such NGOs, many church
related. A nationwide survey by Chulalongkorn University's
Social Research Institute in 1990 of "public interest" NGOs
found seventy-nine in northern Thailand. Between the two
lists, approximately thirty NGOs were identified that were
involved in highland development work. Their annual budget
in the 1988–1990 period came to slightly over 40,000,000
baht (US$1,600,000 at that time) (CUSRI et al. 1990).

The work carried out by the NGOs ranged from relief work
for refugees to education to income enhancement. As small
organizations just getting started, their organizers had the same
enthusiasm found in the CRCDP.

One example from the generation of the 1970s was Tuanchai Dithet, a native of Bangkok who studied political science
at Chulalongkorn University. In 1970, at the end of her first

year of studies, she attended a youth camp in the north including several days at a Lisu village in Mae Taeng, Chiang Mai. She says this changed her life by making her understand that rural areas were the heart of Thai society. A bright student who won awards in school, she changed her priorities from seeking academic excellence to preparing for working in the hills. On graduation she became a volunteer teacher in Pang Sa Village of Mae Chan District in Chiang Rai. She prepared for hill education by studying the methods used at Summerhill School, a progressive, coeducational, residential school in Suffolk, United Kingdom, founded by A. S. Neill in 1921 as a school where students could participate in management and achieve personal freedom. She also read the works of famous Thai Buddhist monks such as Buddhadasa to find ways to approach the local people (Tuanchai 1985, pp. 8–14). Later she worked with the Hill Area Education Program from where her work expanded further. Eventually the Hill Area Foundation was set up to support it. Her work has expanded into drug demand reduction and cooperation with UNDCP in the IDAP (Integrated Drug Abuse Prevention) project. Most recently, she was elected to be a senator from Chiang Rai province in 2000.

Some NGOs worked together with the government and the UN or bilateral projects. Others remained independent. From just a few NGOs, mainly church related like the Karen Baptist Convention, NGOs proliferated. There are now dozens of NGOs run by hill people themselves, some larger such as IMPECT (Inter-Mountain Peoples Education and Culture in Thailand Association) a multi-ethnic network, and smaller ones that might work in a single district or watershed.[1] By

1. This grew out of a project funded by the Dutch NGO, NOVIB, to support Akha students studying in Thai universities and other small projects begun in about 1981.

2001, there are handicraft cooperatives, marketing ventures, and groups dealing with specific social issues. Some are self-supporting and not dependent on overseas funding.

Although lagging behind the royal family and international projects during the 1970s and early 1980s, as Thai government officials gained more experience in the hills, they started to take the lead through drafting the master plans. As knowledge and experience increased, the government took a greater stake in hill work that was reflected by steadily increased budget allocations for their work. Governmental leadership moved from a top-down orientation to a more cooperative and sometimes bottom up orientation (i.e. initiated by the *tambon* councils).

The new NGOs of the 1980s provided creativity, energy, and diversity. Joined by hilltribe leaders, often themselves from the younger generation, these NGOs began to work at the grassroots level with small participatory projects. Their efforts ended up complementing the royal activities and, eventually sometimes joined with the government's move to more participatory work. In later years, certain of the major projects worked closely with NGOs, such as Mae Chaem Integrated Watershed Development Project, which handed over work to CARE International, and the Thai-German Programme, which cooperated with NGOs in drug rehabilitation work.

As this occurred, at the end of the three decades of highland development work, the internationally funded projects found themselves in many ways resembling the new NGO activities. These in turn found themselves close to the philosophy of the Royal Project and the ideas espoused in the NESDB Eighth Plan and the People's Constitution of 1998.

THAI LESSONS IN EMPOWERING
PEOPLE

The role villagers played in highland projects changed considerably from the 1970s to the 1990s. Over these three decades, the highland development initiatives contributed to the increasingly participatory nature of rural work in Thailand. Projects and agencies introduced, often on an ad hoc basis, techniques and processes comprising larger components of villager participation.

Project personnel, often in touch with rural development experts elsewhere in the world where projects were growing more participatory, experimented with ways to bring villagers into the life of project work. NGOs, by their nature more democratic than larger agencies, supported and encouraged this process.

Acquiescence by the villagers gave way to acceptance, then agreement. Some projects hired villagers. Other villagers, with lowland education, returned to work in highland development. All the projects trained local people in various techniques. As the years passed, it was only natural that the role of villagers in the projects expanded and grew more profound.

Empowering local communities became a priority for the Thai government in the late 1980s. Although bottom-up planning had existed in earlier projects, such as in the Hill

Areas Education Project, it was only after many difficult experiences such as seeing the growth of heroin use in the hills, that empowering local communities became a government priority. Even though accepting this participatory approach occurred a decade and a half after being proposed by King Bhumibol Adulyadej, the highland projects still tended to be more participatory than those in the lowlands.

Just as the adoption of rural integrated development occurred only after the Thai government had made this a part of national planning, participatory work occurred after great and parallel changes had taken place in the Thai nation. The move to a People's Constitution and the granting of extensive local authority to the *tambon* councils in the mid 1990s were a part of this process.[1]

In fact the hill people had enjoyed considerable autonomy in Thailand through the 1960s. But after that, a process taking over a decade brought the majority of the hilltribes under government control. In the late 1970s and early 1980s, partly because of insurgent activity in the hills and partly because of existing government structures, officials were unwilling to allow continued autonomy or to involve the people in a participatory planning process.

Nevertheless, a pragmatic approach to solving problems encountered in the hills, changes in Thai society as a whole, and support from international agencies for more participatory work, began to change the focus of Thailand's hill develop-

---

1. *Tambon* councils are local organizations which are invested with considerable administrative authority in local areas according to the Royal Tambon Administrative Organization Act. A *tambon* (sometimes officially translated as "commune") is a cluster of villages administered by a *kamnan* (headman) which comprises a part of a district in the Thai administrative structure.

ment work. Eventually, the participatory approach became government policy.

The participatory process and its introduction into development work in the northern Thai hills has largely escaped the attention of social scientists in academia. Inhibited still perhaps by the old controversy over the Tribal Research Centre and also perhaps not wishing to examine the "applied" phenomenon of the development world, anthropologists concentrated instead on topics such as kinship and social structure, gender roles, religion and tradition, as well as farming and forestry practices.

In some cases, even when a research topic chosen by an anthropologist could be expected to include discussion of development work in the area, social scientists ignored the issue. For example, in Otome Klein Hutheesing's study of emerging sexual inequality among the Lisu in a village in Chiang Rai province, no mention is made that the village is located near Doi Chang in the TG-HDP area. Despite her account of how increasing contact between Lisu people and modern urban society is disadvantaging Lisu women, she avoids discussing the role TG-HDP played in worsening the position of women or efforts by the project to create women's groups in highland villages to overcome problems it helped to create.

Social scientists studying the hill people generally grow sympathetic to the problems they face. Although there is quite a lot of anti-tribal sentiment in popular Thai media and in the earlier manifestations of government policy towards people in the hills (as, for example, non-Thai encroachers of the forest growing illegal substances), the accounts of social scientists are far more supportive. Thai academics who have conducted field research among the hills have produced similarly agreeable accounts.

Accompanying this positive perception of Thai hill people by social scientists is the general understanding that government dealings with the hill people, such as through forestry laws and citizenship regulations, have caused problems for the highlanders. Many modern studies of hill people, such as Tapp (1989) focus on responses to oppressive conditions set by the state. Within this tradition is the work by the Hmong anthropologist Lee (1981) who studied Khun Wang in the early years of UN work. His analysis of the problems faced by the Hmong there, which faulted CRCDP efforts, was the last serious academic assessment of highland development work.

Thus it was that highland development projects and NGO efforts to foster participatory initiatives in the hills went on essentially unstudied by social scientists. As this unfolded, the progress made in involving the people went unnoticed or at least unrecorded. Longstanding biases in academia against development projects were allowed to persist despite the positive steps being taken by some projects in the field.

The attitude of many social scientists thus differed vastly from that of Thai government officials including some academics in this country. Whereas Thai officials generally believed that the government was obliged to better the life of the hill people by providing them with services, such as education and health care, academics mainly continued believing that highland projects were unhelpful. Even this author himself, in an article just published (but drafted in 1993), wrote, "King Chulalongkorn would find [the hill people's] plight appalling...because of the lack of alternatives" for them in Thailand (Renard 2000, p. 80).

In the course of writing this report, I realized that hill people have no alternative but to accept the state in particular and lowland society and "development" in general. Where the hill people were once beyond the reach of valley kingdoms and their rulers, such conditions no longer exist. Just thirty years ago, Kirsten Ewer and Peter Hinton studied different groups of Pwo Karens in remote areas of Uthai Thani and Chiang Mai provinces, respectively, who spoke no Thai. Today, economic and population growth in the lowlands has pushed urbanization outwards towards the most isolated areas in Thailand.

If one accepts the inevitability of this growth, then one must accept that major changes would have reached the hills regardless of the opium replacement projects. And while it might seem appalling that hill people have to undergo such changes, to lose much of their culture, their freedom, and traditional good way of life, these transformations are unavoidable.

Seen in this light, the arrival of the development projects in the hills at a time when these socioeconomic changes had hardly begun to transform the highlands was fortuitous. Despite all the mistakes made by project staff members, the inappropriate innovations, and unjust laws and regulations, the projects brought well-meaning people to the hills to work with the highlanders in order to better their way of life. Because the hills were still relatively open and conditions fluid, when wrongful innovations occurred, the social and ecological systems were usually flexible to absorb them.

In time, as the projects refined their approaches, the work grew increasingly people friendly. New organizations within the hills were established, such as village committees, youth groups, women's groups, credit funds, and rice banks. These involved the people in devising ways for coping with social changes affecting the hills. They were meant to overcome the problems besetting the hill people that social scientists were observing.

But the social scientists were not observing the elaboration of this development process. They were not studying how the projects and the people were working to resolve their conflicts and settle differences with lowland society.

As a result, the findings of this experimental, oftentimes intuitive, process was recorded in reports confined almost entirely within the development community. Since this literature customarily was not collected by librarians in Thailand or elsewhere (including the UN system), information on such innovations remained within the oral tradition of projects themselves and the people implementing them. Furthermore, since discussions of these techniques generally appeared as (boring) official reports, publishers shunned them as commercially unviable.

Nevertheless, it is important to discuss the participatory development models devised in Thailand for use in the hills. That of the Thai-German Highland Development Programme is among the most refined, being the product of eighteen years of operation. The following diagram, adapted from Naret et al., eds. (1997, p. 9) illustrates the model's evolution from the Small Farmer Participation Project and TG's own activities.

Three comments (Naret et al., eds. 1997, pp. 10, 11, 12) show the essence of the participatory approach. In the first, referring to the Hill Area Education Project Ashrams, a tribal elder commented that "Thai-German works like the Non-Formal Education Department; it teaches the villagers to think more skillfully." In the second, a TG field station worker asked, "Do we want to see them improve or not?" The third, also by a TG worker, noted that "It is not only us that want to study or evaluate the villagers—the villagers are also evaluating us."

The main purpose of the participatory approach is to develop local human and institutional resources which can then deal with drug abuse and other problems. The approach devised by TG-HDP comprised the steps discussed below.

Figure 3

EVOLUTION OF THE PARTICIPATORY WORKING APPROACH

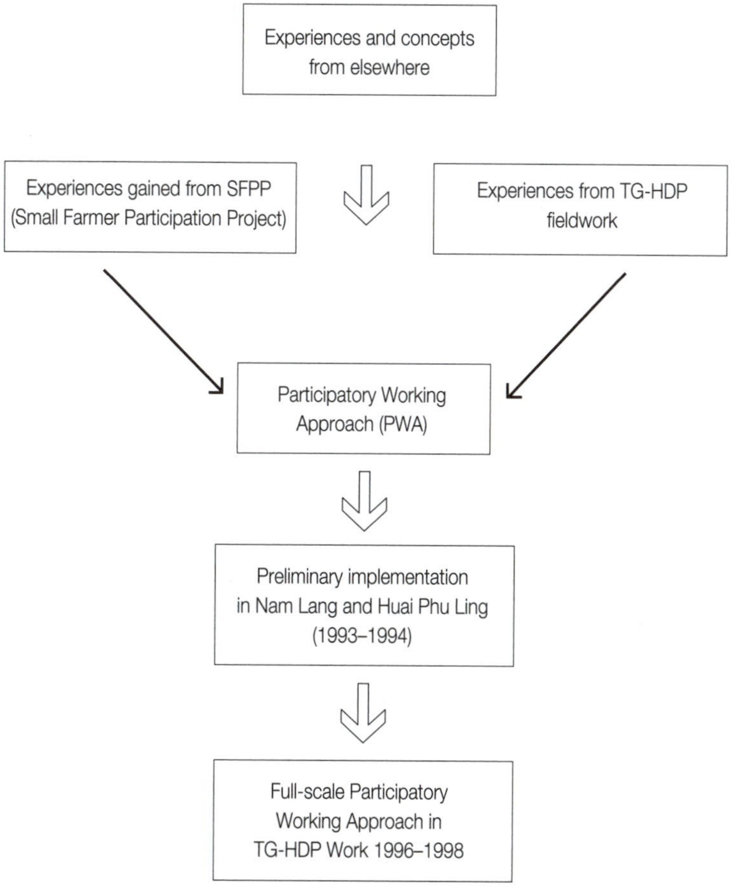

1. Preparation by the Initiator[2]

Initiators should treat the villagers as intellectual equals. Initiators must expect that they can learn from the people with whom they will be working. Although the initiator may know various techniques and have access to much outside information, the local people in Thailand possess a store of indigenous wisdom that can be of much benefit to the development process.

Anthropologists who have worked with hill people in Thailand have reported rich systems of traditional lore. To cite just two examples, Alting (1983) described the Akha system of knowledge called the *Akhazang* while Radley (1986) reviewed the profound cosmology of the Hmong. Soil scientists and others have described sophisticated and sustainable cropping systems maintained by Karens and others, sometimes in the same place for centuries. Their tribal jungle lore, ranging from a knowledge of pharmaceutical preparations to hunting skills to handicraft abilities, has been long respected by their neighbors. The languages of some groups are of remarkable linguistic complexity while the oral literature provides rich material for study.

2. Building Familiarity

Once the initiator accepts that the local people have a rich culture, building familiarity should be straightforward. This starts with treating the villagers respectfully and humanely, being punctual, and honoring decisions made by the people.

Sometimes small projects which can show immediate results build familiarity quickly. During the 1980 baseline survey of Tha Pha and Chang Khoeng *tambons* of the Mae Chaem

---

2. UNDCP projects prefer the term "initiator" which lacks some of the implied top-down orientation of "developer."

Project, a member of the team suggested to USAID that small projects with immediate results would be appreciated by the villagers. Within the year, a special fund was established to fund small projects. Most of these consisted of irrigation repairs and improvements with the purpose of increasing the village rice supply (Keen 1984, p. 5). Many similar examples can be cited, often involving water supplies.[3]

3. Community Analysis

Once mutual trust is established, the community's strengths and weaknesses are evaluated by the Participatory Rural Appraisal (PRA). Popularized by Robert Chambers and his colleagues who have written voluminously on the subject, PRA enables both residents and initiators of a community to mobilize development activities (for an example regarding health, see Chambers 1992).

A wide range of techniques has been identified to collect information on rural communities including those with many non-literate people. Basically, small teams are set up to map the village, sometimes using stones and twigs for better understanding by people not comfortable using written symbols or words. Rural systems are assessed and ways are identified to make them more effective.

Care should be taken to establish a framework for data collection that can be shared with other initiatives. Once the data is collected using the diverse techniques that comprise the PRA approach, initiators should take care to define categories, such as age group, time intervals, and income levels, in a way that data sharing with other places can readily be done.

---

3. Clean water delivery using such innovations as filters or distribution pipes are inexpensive and show immediate results, reducing disease, saving labor, and enhancing cleanliness.

All the data collected belongs to the villagers. Sharing it and discussing it with them enables them to be fully involved in the assessment process. Iterative processes are used to review situations and problems thoroughly.[4]

4. Group Processes

PRA supports working cooperatively. Existing groups in a village can be involved in PRAs or new ones can be established. New groups can also be set up as a part of solving problems in the village. Sometimes this has included helping the government to establish village committees. Groups established include textile weaving cooperatives or community-based drug treatment groups. TG's work on the latter is discussed below. TG-HDP provided considerable assistance in creating new groups, training leaders, and helping the groups operate effectively.

5. Leadership and Network Development

Moving beyond village level work to establishing networks leads to productive change. Once groups in individual villages were established, TG encouraged them to work together with similar groups in other communities to form networks. Networks enable villagers to make use of the expertise of leaders in other communities. To make sure the networks functioned over the long-term, TG made special efforts to train leaders of networks and prepare future leaders. Because there was little experience in villages of network operations this was a time-consuming process.

---

4. Many PRA techniques have been identified that will enable this to be done quickly and economically. UN and other projects in neighboring MOU (Memorandum of Understanding) countries have followed this basic approach, including the Wa Project in Myanmar, the Palaveck and Nong Het Projects in the Lao PDR, and the Ky Son Project in Vietnam.

Figure 4
PROCESSES OF COMMUNITY-BASED DRUG ABUSE CONTROL
(CB-DAC)

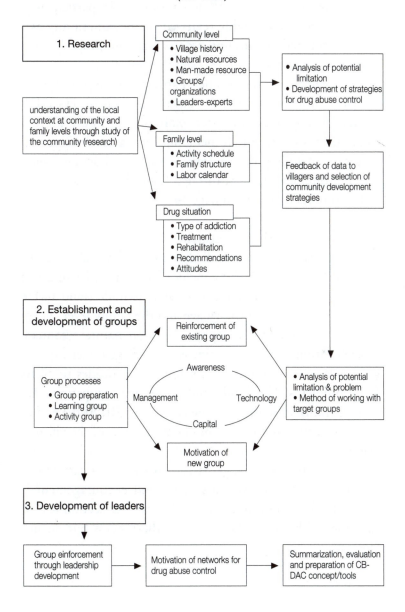

6. The Action Reflection Process

Monitoring and evaluation of the participatory process ensures its sustainability. All activities done in participatory work should be thoroughly reviewed by the community as a whole. If this action reflection process functions properly, then the entire participatory process should work too.

In implementing the people's participatory approach with special attention to community-based drug control, TG-HDP reduced the process to three main steps. These are: 1) community study/research including rural analysis, 2) group processes, including preparatory, learning and acting stages, and 3) group development through leadership development.

The process is shown on page 145.

1. Community Study/Research

Drug abuse should be studied as a part of overall community conditions. TG-HDP concluded that in order to assess the drug abuse situation, it was necessary to understand a wide range of topics at both the village and the family level. These included food and opium poppy cultivation, natural resources, village relations with the outside world, village leadership and social relations, community wisdom, and attitudes to all its major problems. The family study examined occupational activities, family structure, and the labor calendar. At the end of the study, drugs may or may not be seen as one of the village's major problems.

Although this is a village-based process, when carried out for the first time, outside assistance and encouragement is required. The project initiators in the previous section (called "developers" by TG-HDP) support the process but do not direct it.

2. Group Processes

As defined by TG-HDP, this step comprises the creation of a core group of leaders who recognize village problems, accept that these problems are their own, and are prepared to take steps to solve them. If the villagers do not identify drug abuse as a problem they must solve, there is little hope of reducing drug use there. As shown in figure 4, this is a three-step process.

In the preparatory group stage, once a core group of leaders is identified, community meetings are held. In this process, there are three goals:

1) the community becomes aware of the problems caused by drug addiction,
2) community groups commit themselves to solve drug problems, and
3) users realize the problems they cause.

To this can be added a lesson learned by the villagers as noted by Anek and Suwannarat (1994). They observe that "the critical addict component is personal intention to discontinue drug use and receive detoxification, ensuring greater post-treatment success. There is also need for different models to be applied in diverse conditions depending on whether the village has strong or weak leadership, is factionalized (such as by different religions), is located near trafficking routes, or produces rice (Chayan et al. 1997, pp. 44–45). If all this can be accomplished, the village can move to the next stage.

In the first stage, the villagers study their own community, learning what group process means and beginning to carry it out. Through village forums and other activities such as, for example, study tours, the villagers prepare a workplan to control drug use. Sometimes fundraising is also carried out.

Once the plan is prepared, the village is ready for the action group stage when the workplan activities are implemented. Assistance can be provided by the government or NGOs as appropriate. The community should monitor the activities conducted and evaluate them frequently so as to be able to make adjustments when required. As a part of the monitoring process, different groups in the village are encouraged to exchange experiences.

3. Group Development through Leadership Development

As the groups in the community conduct activities, the leadership in the groups develops. This strengthens the entire group process and the organization of networks which solve problems more efficiently.

The process is working if the community is:

1) taking action to reduce drug problems,
2) improving the village environment,
3) controlling other vices,
4) promoting sports and vocational activities,
5) establishing and encouraging youth groups,
6) exchanging experiences with other activities, and
7) establishing inter-village drug abuse control networks.

IMPACT ANALYSIS OF ALTERNATIVE DEVELOPMENT

Analyses of the impact of assistance in alternative development have been made regularly since the 1970s. Major reviews were made in the mid 1990s when UNDCP funding largely came to a halt with the completion of most of the highland development projects.

One significant evaluation was by a team headed by Robert Moreland (Moreland et al. 1993). In 1994, when the UNDCP Projects Coordination Office in Chiang Mai closed a seminar was organized by ONCB and UNDCP on "Two Decades of Thai-UN Cooperation in Highland Development and Drug Control." Five papers presented covered participatory land-use planning (Uraivan et al), sustainable agriculture (Kanok), the development of community institutions and networks (Chaiwat), health and education (Renard et al.), and drug treatment (Anek and Suwannarat).

Moreland et al (1993, pp. 49–56) notes the following major impacts on the target populations:

1) Decreased opium production and use; increased heroin availability,
2) Good progress in rural development,
3) Greater stress on environment because alternative crops

need larger growing areas and more chemical inputs than opium poppy,

4) Positive impact on standard of living, acceptable decline in self-reliance,

5) Reinforced village organizational structures.

6) Improved skills in functioning in Thai society (despite lack of UNDCP placing tribal people in decision-making positions in projects),

7) Enhanced capacity of the Thai government drug control and policy development.

They also noted that coordination between projects was poor despite the existence of a Projects Coordination Office (PCO) in Chiang Mai that was established to encourage such communication. Related to this, they noted that:

There is no comprehensive and/or reliable data base, either in scope or chronological, which permits definitive statements on most individual projects or the collective UNDCP-supported effort. In many cases the data bases differ among projects and, thus, neither comparisons between projects nor overall summaries can be made...[although] trends and impacts [can be indicated] (Moreland et al. 1993, annex 2).

The evaluators also noted that the PCO had managed to improve relations among projects, NGOs, and the academic community even though these lay outside the PCO's normal responsibilities.

The papers delivered at the PCO seminar in 1994 largely agreed with the seven conclusions by Moreland et al. noted above. Anek and Suwannarat suggested community-based responses to increased heroin use (conclusion 1, above). Uraivan et al. showed how land use planning in the Sam Mun Highland Development Project had promoted rural development and environmental protection (2, 3). Kanok concluded that hill agriculture had become more sustainable (3, 4). Renard et al. discussed improved health and education services in the hills (4). Chaiwat described improving community institutions and networks that (together with a Thai education) facilitated the hill functioning in Thai society (5, 6). Conclusion 7 was not discussed specifically in any of the papers and not identified as problematic.

Regarding data, Renard et al (pp. 2–3) observed that good socioeconomic and demographic data is essential. "Categories of data collection (such as age groups, village clusters, time intervals) must be well-defined and used at all phases in each and for every project run in a country."[1]

IMPACT OF OPIUM REPLACEMENT ON HEROIN USE

The impact of alternative development on opium eradication is well documented as discussed in chapter 5 of this report. Less well understood are the factors contributing to the increased heroin use in the highlands that occurred in the mid 1980s when active poppy eradication began.

Looking at the situation broadly, many have concluded that as the supply of opium declined, the users turned to heroin. Since heroin takes up only 10 percent of the space of a comparable amount of opium and is a dry odorless powder it can be smuggled much easier. There are cases in history where such a transition has been made. Although there is some truth

---

1. This was not the case in the Thai alternative development experience where quantitative data collection categories were not always maintained even within the same project.

to this generalization, the details of the transition from using opium to heroin in the Thai hills indicates such a scenario is not inevitable.

A key event occurred sometime in the mid 1980s when the Hmong learned how to refine heroin. The exact date of this technological transfer is not known but it should not have been earlier than 1985 when increased heroin use in the highlands was first observed. Although it cannot be determined whether this transfer took place because of the increased opium poppy destruction, it occurred at the time when the opiate supply in Thailand declined.

Although the transfer of refining technology to the Hmong presumably made heroin more affordable, using it still required cash. This encouraged the spread of heroin use to villages in project areas where there was increased income principally because of the crops promoted there. The spread, as usual for drugs, went along trafficking routes which would have gone to the old opium growing sites such as Mae Sa Mai in Chiang Mai province where the first major heroin outbreak was observed. It is likely too, as Moreland et al (1993, p. 50) note, that traffickers were increasing their marketing activities in the mid 1980s. This allowed them to introduce heroin to a younger group of people, generally men who were economically active and more open to experimentation.

As this occurred, the UNFDAC projects gave little warning of possible change in drug use. Contributing to this was an unbalanced approach.

Too much emphasis was placed on crop replacement. Because CRCDP and HAMP arose more out of concern by the American government than the Thai government, the project objectives were supply reduction so drugs would not be exported from Thailand. Much less attention was given to local users. Agricultural experts dominated the staff of the early projects. Thus, little thought was given to creating warning systems to alert project officials to drug use changes.

In Thailand and elsewhere including UNFDAC, drug control was in the early 1980s primarily a law enforcement operation. What attention was given to demand reduction was to rehabilitate users in lowland centers where recidivism was high. Almost no drug prevention activities were included in the early projects.

Partly this is because there were few specialists in drug demand control worldwide in the 1980s. Few programs existed for demand reduction in general and almost none for rural areas or indigenous peoples. The body of information that could be used in dealing with drug-using populations in the highlands of Thailand had yet to be assembled.

Problems of heroin use in rural populations were new not just to Thailand but to the world. It can be concluded, as Moreland et al. note, that the spread of heroin in the hills "occurred independently of the overall rural development effort and clearly can not be attributed to the UNDCP, or other projects alone" (1993, p. 51).

As described above, the UN, the development projects, and the Thai government all revised their approach to drug use to take a more balanced approach by the early 1990s. ONCB's policy no longer singles out individual drugs as targets but attempts to counter the entire drug using culture. In a project undertaken with the Ministry of Education in Thailand (and in cooperation with a UNDCP subregional demand reduction project on high-risk groups), a package for dealing with the entire issue of deviant behavior is being prepared, of which drug use is but one part.

IMPACT OF OPIUM REPLACEMENT ON HILL COMMUNITIES

The impact of alternative development on overall economic changes in the hills must be analyzed within the entire highland context in the last three decades.

The development process has been blamed for causing the loss of tribal culture and traditions. Going to Thai schools, it is contended, creates an environment "where tribespeople become ashamed of their roots." Kampe (1992, p. 163) and Moreland et al. (1993, annex 2) note that hill people with lowland educations sometimes do not function in their native community or in Thai society.

There are forces, however, larger than the development process related to crop replacement. Regardless of international donors or even the existence of opium in the hills, eventually the growing Thai economy and population would have begun entering the hills. Roads and other infrastructure developments would have gone into the highlands guided almost purely by private enterprise, the forces of globalization, and laissez-faire.

By the end of the 1990s, when the development paradigm had become participatory, the chance for villagers to practice their culture began to be reestablished. Indigenous textile and other handicraft production grew to reach a growing market. Local leadership found new authority through the *tambon* council and was in a position to promote the strengths of local culture. Educated tribal people are also finding productive niches for themselves in Thai life as teachers, NGO workers, and sometimes in private enterprise.

The development process discussed here, comprising royal initiatives, internationally funded projects, NGO work, and Thai governmental plans, took three decades to reach its final form. Hundreds of millions of dollars were expended in the effort. By the end of the process, (and not ignoring problems that occurred in the formative process), a development model was created for the socioeconomic development of the highlands.

Alternative development did not create Thailand's highland policy, but since crop replacement work began at the same time that the government was beginning to develop a policy for working with the hilltribes, there was considerable influence. This influence extended particularly over the three "problem" areas identified by the Department of Public Welfare in its 1964–1969 five-year plan: opium cultivation, socioeconomic development, forest and watershed destruction, and possible lack of loyalty to Thailand.

1. Facilitating Forest Use

The viability of the forests under shifting cultivation notwithstanding, according to Royal Forest Acts since at least 1938, forests could not be inhabited. Adhering to this law implied that people living in forests would have to be resettled elsewhere. This was clearly impossible for the hundreds of thousands of hill people already living in forests.

Even before the start of CRCDP, project planners and some government officials recognized that without a system giving the hill people some land tenure rights, crop replacement would fail. No hill person would make the effort to grow new crops if they faced the risk of being evicted before they could profit from it.

Throughout the history of the highland projects various techniques were used to give the hill people access to the forest. The Sam Mun Project, in which the Royal Forest Department was the executing agency, pioneered participatory land use planning. Almost all the projects experimented with different cropping systems in the difficult quest to replace opium poppy cultivation with other sustainable agricultural practices.

Such efforts have figured prominently in the development of the community forest concept and the drafting of the Community Forestry Bill. Through efforts by the highland projects, NGOs, and some governmental agencies (also because there is little appropriate land on which they can be settled), various land use practices have been legitimized in the hills and very few groups of hill people have been forced to relocate. Within the Royal Forest, proponents of community forestry, some with UN project experience, dominate the Community Forestry Division.

2. Providing Citizenship

Beginning with CRCDP, all the projects sought ways to legitimize the existence of the hill people in Thailand. Government regulations regarding residence location and documentation as well as other factors impeded these efforts. One important constraint was a Ministry of Interior regulation penalizing government officials who granted citizenship to aliens who then engaged in illegal activities. Another constraint was that applications had to be signed by very high officials in the Ministry.

Various short-term solutions were found. Persons who could prove they had lived in Thailand for a certain number of years were in some cases given permits to reside and work in the border province they were located. Some individuals, particularly Karens, who as a group had lived in Thailand for much longer (and who did not grow much opium) found it easier to obtain citizenship than such peoples as the Hmong, Yao, Lisu, Akha, and Lahu (who did grow opium).

Eventually in early 2000, the Department of Local Administration revised its methodology for granting citizenship giving considerable authority to the district officer. In the last ten months, thousands of hill people have received citizenship. The contribution of the alternative development projects to this process cannot be quantified but it was substantial.

3. Planning for Hill Development

The alternative development projects focussed attention on the hills. When there were problems of inter-agency competition and jealousies in the 1970s, the government responded by drafting master plans for highland development. Had the crop replacement and highland development projects not existed there may well have been no such effort. In drafting the master plans, experts from the projects and Thai officials with experience in highland work played a significant role. As a result, not only did the alternative development initiatives spur the creation of master plans but those who had gained experience in the work shaped the form the plans took.

4. Providing Infrastructure

When alternative development work started in the early 1970s, virtually no infrastructure in the hills existed. Few roads entered the highlands and there were all but no schools, clinics, agricultural stations, or other government outposts in the northern hills. When projects began in the hills and drew attention to the people there, the government resolved to provide more services. Roads, health clinics, electricity and water supply facilities, and schools all were provided through the implementation of the hill master plans. This did not change national policy but hastened implementation. Some of this would have happened as the economy grew and government capacity grew, but the highland projects hastened the process.

A distinction must be made between project work and unrelated changes in the hills. Activities as unrelated as cabbage marketing, heroin use, village relocation, and commercial sex work by hilltribe youth have been attributed to highland projects. But there is a limit to the effect these projects have had.

In the 1970s when the Thai Third Army spent more time in firefights with hill people than in cooperating with them in development work, the UN projects and the Royal Project were the only influential friends the hill people had. Although the projects accelerated contacts between lowland and highland society, sometimes resulting in harm to the latter, such contacts were inevitable.

It was better for the hill people that projects specifically trying to improve conditions for the hilltribes reached them before other projects. Although the project teams were inexperienced in hill work and unfamiliar with the highland customs, they were nonetheless trying to work with the hill people to create a higher standard of living. Commercial developers and individual investors were also unfamiliar with the hills but were working to create a higher standard living for themselves, not for the hilltribes.

SUSTAINING ALTERNATIVE
DEVELOPMENT EFFORTS

Sustainability in Thailand was accomplished through coop-eration among many agencies in the government, international organizations, and the people. At the start of the process, national security concerns made it difficult for development agencies to work in certain areas. By the 1980s, the suppres-sion of insurgencies turned to motivating the people, and such areas as Yao/Pha Mon, on the Lao border in Chiang Rai and the site of insurgent activity, became integrated into the devel-opment process.

Seven factors have contributed to the sustainability of alternative development work in Thailand. The first three involve working with the people. These coincide with steps identified by King Bhumibol through his own experiences in development. He believes that people accept and implement activities through a natural and continuing development cycle. These first three he believes lead to sustainable innovation adoption (RDPB 1997, pp. 286–291). Examples of how this was actually accomplished are given for each point.

Interspersed with these comments are observations made by General Chavalit Yodmani, secretary general of ONCB from 1983–1995 who has had considerable experience in control-ling opium in Thailand. Trained at the Eaton Hall Officer's

Cadet School, the Hendon Detective School, and New Scotland Yard in the United Kingdom, General Chavalit's early career was in the foreign affairs section of the Thai police. He became Thailand's key mobilizer for two decades (ONCB 1995; Chavalit Interview 2000).

1. Public Awareness

Spreading information is essential to sustainable development. Lessons learned in one place have to be retained and shared. Systems have to be created by which appropriate information is stored and also made available to everyone who can make use of it, including villagers, government officials, and persons in the international development community.

An example from the Sam Mun Project village of Pang Khum shows how disseminating information can resolve difficulties. Pang Khum was a village with Karen, northern Thai, and Lisu residents. There were imbalances in land ownership. The Karens who had settled there first possessed the most. The Northern Thai had settled here later, often intermarrying with the Karens and they too owned considerable land. The Lisu who arrived afterwards had fewer land holdings forcing them to clear the forest to grow food and some opium, and to herd cattle. The cattle often escaped their grazing area and fed in the Karen and northern Thai swidden and paddy fields. The northern Thai and Karen dominated village leadership and contacts with the government. The Lisu responded by refusing to participate in official meetings which exacerbated their position.

The project responded by organizing a participatory land use planning (PLP) process (based on the Participatory Rural Appraisal (PRA)). A Chiang Mai University anthropology professor and UNDCP evaluator describes the process:

PLP strategies focussed on opening up information to the villagers so that they would understand each others' farming systems and constraints they each faced. To this end, contour maps were essential in showing the wide range in land ownership. A crucial point in the process came when a wealthy Karen leader publicly acknowledged that many Lisu did not have enough land to survive. Frequent meetings were held to show people the source of problems and promote open discussion of and agreement about ways to solve these problems. Special attention had to be paid to encouraging Lisu to attend meetings.

Ultimately, a small-scale land reallocation was carried out by RFD [Royal Forest Department[1]]. . . The conflict within Pang Khum made it necessary to have another authority [i.e. the Sam Mun Project and the RFD] carry out the allocation —there was no indigenous network uniting the Karen and Lisu within which land reallocation could have taken place. At the same time, however, work was being done to create institutions for villagers to work together (Uraivan et al. 1994, pp. 39–40).

General Chavalit added that working with youth is important. When the development process started, most addicts were older. One of the lessons learned in Thailand, so obvious now that most people have forgotten that it had to be learned, was that projects should work to evoke a love for the land among young highlanders so that they will cooperate in development work.

1. The RFD was the executing agency of the project for the Thai government.

2. Public Interest

King Bhumibol Adulyadej gives catchy titles to his projects to attract attention. "Salt Roads," for example, was a project by which the source of salt to Samoeng district of Chiang Mai province was traced back to its origin on the Gulf of Thailand. This project then arranged for salt at the beginning of the road to be iodized to prevent goiter at the road's end in Samoeng. The project titles attract attention making it possible for people to learn more.

A wide range of techniques have been used by agencies to evoke interest. The Royal Project adopted the trade name of Doi Kham which has served it well. Signs, advertisements, and other media have introduced other activities in other spheres.

Interest is also provoked by actively supporting the people. In the Thai-Norwegian Project village of Pha Daeng, in Lampang province, several of the Yao villagers went to the lowlands to sell opium. On arriving at the assigned meeting place at a waterfall, the "buyers" told them the deal had to be made in Wang Nua town, a few kilometers off. Even though the village headman grew suspicious and refused to go, most of the other menfolk did ride to Wang Nua where they were promptly arrested. TN-HDP lobbied on behalf of the villagers saying that a "sting" of this sort undermined the integrity of the project. Besides, most of those remaining in the village were women who could not make a satisfactory living on their own. Eventually an early release was arranged, an event that evoked considerable confidence in the project among the villagers.[2]

2. In 1990, the government established the Doi Luang National Park. Because Pha Daeng was located within the park, the villagers had to be relocated. This was the kind of event beyond the projects' control that could betray the villagers' trust and upset overall highland development.

3. Time for Evaluation and Trial Periods

Creating self-reliance takes time. Royally sponsored initiatives allow for the people to get to know the guidelines slowly. When King Bhumibol suggested it would take three decades to replace opium, he was allowing for new concepts to be introduced at the people's pace.

Although such long timeframes may seem impossible for highland projects, the Thai-German Highland Development Programme existed for eighteen years. The participatory approach it used so well only reached its full development in the last five years. Projects with a life of three to five years, common for the UN, can succeed only under highly favorable and unusual conditions.

Although the plan was for government agencies to take over the work started by the UN, this has rarely been successful.

Yao women, Pha Daeng village, Lampang

Ronald D. Renard

Budgetary allocations, changes in government priorities, and other factors have interrupted the smooth transfer of project work. NGOs can play a key role—CARE International took over some of the work of the Mae Chaem Project in 1989 where it still works, sometimes dealing with new problems.

Perhaps the most sustainable approach was taken by the Thai-German Programme. TG-HDP sought to strengthen local leadership through the *tambon* council and other local agencies supported by the new constitution. TG-HDP promoted local networks and enhanced village leadership capacity so that the people themselves would be empowered to work with the government and the private sector. An example from Ya Pa Nae village in Mae Hong Son illustrates the usefulness of a long-term approach.

This Lahu village lay on the border opposite a caravan route controlled by Khun Sa. A large opium refinery had been set up in a neighboring village. Opiate use in the village was high. The project sent dozens of users for treatment in Chiang Mai, but many relapsed. In 1983, TG-HDP identified Ya Pa Nae as a target village in dealing with drug use. Project staff analyzed past efforts to reduce drug use, concluding that the Village Committee (itself set up through TG-HDP efforts) had not made a commitment to solve the problem. To help the discouraged TG-HDP staff in the village, the Project made a renewed effort by strengthening the village groups that it had helped to set up in the first place. The field staff encouraged the people's organizations to "reevaluate and improve their role in the village by inviting them to evaluate the data from the community and network studies." Some of the groups were overhauled and the new members decided that

3. A word with no precise parallel in English, *parami* denotes grace, loving kindness, charisma, stature, power, and greatness.

drug use had to be controlled. When the new evaluations succeeded, the TG field staff decided to strengthen the women's and youth groups so that they could play a role in drug control as well (Pairote and Orapin 1998, pp. 63–65).

4. Visionary Leadership

Thailand was fortunate that King Bhumibol Adulyadej had been promoting environmentally friendly, participatory projects, and people-driven work even before the development community "devised" these guidelines. As a constitutional monarch above politics, he devoted his considerable energies to helping the people. The common folk of the country, who recognized in him high levels of *parami* [3] and empathy for their living conditions, cooperated fully.

Continually, his message was one of supporting the high-landers. He used his influence over different government agencies such as the Royal Forest Department and other units in the Ministries of Interior and Agriculture to encourage them to assist the poppy growers. This was particularly helpful in cases where existing regulations, usually drafted for people in the lowlands, impeded the government from helping the hill people.

Through this leadership, government agencies, NGOs, and people's organizations found inspiration. As they gained strength and expertise they gradually accepted guidelines established by King Bhumibol Adulyadej.

5. National Unity and Political Will

Thailand is structurally unified. The educational system has created shared values, cultural oneness, and a willingness to accept government policies. The king symbolizes this unity. Once the government decided to eradicate opium, the people and government complied. In the 1980s, when overlapping mandates created difficulties, or in the 1990s when various approaches were devised, the goal was not forgotten.

In the 1960s, the military governments controlled the country politically when the business community was not sufficiently strong to mount a challenge, and democratic or student movements were still in a formative stage. Shared values learned in school predisposed a general willingness to accept government policies. The king's rule symbolized the unity of the people.

The people readily supported the decision to eradicate opium in the hills. Made illegal over a decade earlier, opium had no supporters and few users in the lowlands. In the 1980s, when the overlapping mandates of different agencies created difficulties, the government established highland development master plans under which NGOs and government agencies participated with the goal of opium reduction intact.

In the 1990s, Thailand had experienced fifty years of economic development and political unity. Confident Thai leaders allowed the country's "Thai" nationalism to start encompassing other cultures. This allowed the participatory process to expand into the hills without threatening national unity. Through this, General Chavalit noted that the government also created confidence and a sense of security among the hill people that they could make a productive living in peace.

6. Commitment of Ample Resources

Besides the many highland development projects funded by international donors, the government allocated increasing sums of money for developing the hills. NGOs, both domestic and overseas, contributed additional sums. In all, the investment in opium replacement and related highland development activities by royal projects, international donors, NGOs, and the government was over one billion U.S. dollars.

Economically, to invest this much in eliminating the production of perhaps 100 tons of opium per year makes no sense. But if one considers, as did the drafters of the Mae Chaem project, that opium cultivation was an indicator of poverty and that overall development would reduce poppy growing in the process, then it can be seen as worthwhile. An unintended consequence of the opium replacement effort was to involve a team of people basically dedicated to helping the hill people achieve a better life.

The commitment of the funds for development occurred as the government pushed the frontier back from the lowlands into the hills. Infrastructure such as roads, schools, health stations, and irrigation projects were built in the hills. Thailand's booming economy in the 1980s and early 1990s enabled it to devote large amounts of resources to highland initiatives.

Among these resources is information and data that must be shared. General Chavalit observed that project work requires accurate information on the people and their environment. Those managing the development process must retain this information so that later project personnel and younger villagers can use it. Data bases once compiled in a standardized way must be updated and continually available for use.

7. Participation of the People

The people worked willingly with the projects to replace opium. But only in Phase Three did the projects become genuinely participatory. General Chavalit said that a bottom-up approach was required. Not giving away things for free, he said, helped in this because it kept the villagers from taking the project for granted. Even then the involvement of the people in their affairs spread unevenly because of vested interests and continued distrust of the highlanders. As villages grow more participatory and more people join in local initiatives, their resilience will grow along with their resistance to drug use.

CONCLUSIONS AND RECOMMENDATIONS

Where the need is greatest, a visionary leadership, an inclusive unity towards a national goal, and strong international funding are now harder to find. However, the Thai example represents an historical milestone, a process of successful and complex change, achieved peacefully with high people participation and satisfaction (Calvani 2000, p. 4).

As shown on the table following this section, the three-phase process began in 1969. Through the process, a comprehensive model for working in the highlands of northern Thailand emerged.

At this time, Thai officials had little knowledge about drug use, poppy cultivation, addiction and its treatment. Few Thais knew the hills or their people. The country's agricultural expertise and legal system was based on life in the lowland valleys. Citizenship, forestry and other laws based on lowland life constituted actual constraints to highland development in areas where ethnic minorities made a living in hill area forests. The process is outlined in table 9 (p. 174).

For the first phase, during the 1970s, the highland development projects were donor driven, aiming at replacing opium as a cash crop. Although basically agreeing with the direction of the projects, neither the government nor the people were active stakeholders. The prevailing philosophy of the projects was law enforcement which was only one-third of the alternative development package.

During the second phase in the 1980s, integrated rural development projects were carried out. In this, the government participated with the donors, but the people were still not actively engaged. The combination of law enforcement (eradication beginning in this phase) and community development constituted two-thirds of the alternative development package. Because of its incompleteness, communities were left vulnerable to new threats such as heroin addiction, which grew quickly.

In the third phase that coincides approximately with the 1990s, the donors, government, and people participated. All three components of alternative development: law enforcement, community development, and demand reduction were present. So effective has this complete model been that opium production cartels have reportedly started using Thailand as an experimental area where they virtually have to bribe growers to plant opium poppy.

Not all who view this process admire it, however. Such observers point out that the total amount of opium reduction in Thailand is only a small percentage of the total amount grown in the region. Many opium growers, they say, have simply moved across the border to neighboring countries where cultivation has increased much more than it has declined in Thailand (Moreland et al. 1993, annex 2). Others noted that the use of other drugs: heroin, and ATS, has grown so much that there are more addicts in the hills than before.

But at the end of the process, a highland development model was created. The model comprises a balanced approach that can control new and existing drug use. The participatory nature of the model facilitates local initiatives and community-based work in drug control, development, and the expression of local culture.

Thailand has achieved impressive results of opium eradication in the past thirty years: the approach, once devised, was straightforward, comprising the involvement of the people in law enforcement, community development, and demand reduction. The leadership of King Bhumibol Adulyadej, strong political will, national unity, together with the sound investment of the international community and the Thai government, were major factors.

This is a recipe that might be difficult to export to other countries now entangled in complex policies and debates on using alternative development to eliminate illicit crops. Nevertheless, the Thai model is the basis for highland projects by UN, bilateral, and some international NGO projects in Laos, Vietnam, and Myanmar.

One need in this process is to increase the flow of information about the hill people. The need to collect information on the hill people was recognized long ago when plans were laid for setting up the Tribal Research Centre. The need has been officially recognized by United Nations organizations, particularly in the resolution adopted by the General Assembly in 1998.[1] This called for giving "due regard to the dissemination of information on the situation, cultures, languages, rights and aspirations of indigenous people."

This information flow begins with data collected by the villagers on their own conditions. Such data should be stored according to how the villagers interpret it, as well as according to the categories used throughout the region. Age groups (such

1. The resolution appears in the report of the Third Committee (A/52/641) regarding the International Decade of the World's Indigenous People.

as of addicts), duration (such as how long someone must stay off drugs to say that person is rehabilitated) and other such categories must be established and maintained in a consistent and area-wide system.[2]

Information, whether stored in a library or made available to policymakers, still constitutes a flow out of the village that does nothing directly to better the local way of life. Indigenous villagers throughout the region know that there is information useful to them on all types of subjects from specific crops, to drug treatment methodologies, to village fund formation to which they have no access. They are aware of advances in communication, publications, and information exchange, all of which they want to participate in.

To make this information flow succeed, then, the information should first be available to the communities where it was generated. The participatory process mandates that the people, including poppy growers and other marginalized people such as drug users, can use this information. Projects must find innovative ways to make this happen.

Projects should also identify ways to share information generated elsewhere in other times. All too often information is treated as confidential during the life of a project and then discarded when the project is completed.[3] Many such agencies treat reports as a necessary evil to meet bureaucratic require-

---

2. This was never done in Thailand. The rush for results, the lack of a central hill area administrative agency, the diversity of executing agencies, and the lengthiness of projects were contributing factors in inconsistencies in data collection, which sometimes occurred even between different phases of the same project.

3. At the end of CRCDP, Richard Mann was told to destroy all the UN records he had. He kept some, though, which are now the only remaining copies.

ments. The culture of many UN agencies downplays the role of the written word, preferring to work with people directly. But as people are transferred or retire and as projects are concluded, the lessons learned are too easily lost or forgotten. The UN, local governments, and other agencies must revise their institutional history of forgetfulness and create means for storing and sharing data. On-line systems can help, but hard copies or microfilmed records are important as backup.

Ways must then be found to make all the relevant information available to the people. They know that the information era is leaving them behind. Language differences, illiteracy, and poor storage facilities are obstacles that agencies of all types must overcome.

One sign of development and self-sufficiency is a lively cultural literature. Communities and peoples in decline rarely have a thriving literature. In the northern Thai hills, the oral literature of the people is almost universally in decline. Accounts of the hill people are now written more by people from Bangkok and anthropologists from elsewhere in the world. Little new oral literature is being composed and most learning now comes from schools and Thai national media. Reflecting this, in 1986, a young Hmong in Mae Chon village, just outside the Thai-Norwegian Project area, said, "everything in Hmong society was inferior to everything in Thai society." Far from preserving their cultural identity, Karen migrants to Chiang Mai city often respond to the questions of surveyors with "Who told you I was Karen?"

Although the fault for this lack of confidence and complacency may not have lain with the development projects, they are in a good position to overcome it. Work should be undertaken with indigenous groups, particularly large networks such as IMPECT. In one project, with support from UNICEF and Chiang Mai's provincial primary education authorities,

Table 9

THE EVOLUTION OF DRUG CONTROL POLICY AND ALTERNATIVE DEVELOPMENT (AD) IN THAILAND

GLOBAL TRENDS	THAI TRENDS	THAI DRUG CONTROL POLICY	HIGHLAND WORK PRIORITIES
	1957: Opiates outlawed	Law enforcement	Benign neglect
1965+: Drug use in West grows/ Political youth movements	1961: NESDB 5-year plans		Suppress insurgencies Resettlement in lowlands
	1971: Golden Triangle political youth movement	1969: HM into hills Royal Project	
		1971: Thailand agrees for first UNFDAC country office to be set up in Bangkok	**AD 1. 1970s Crop Replacement**
	14 October 1973–6 October 1976: Youth in resistance	1976: ONCB established	*Donor participation Law enforcement
		1980s: Highland master plans	**AD 2. 1980s Integrated Rural Development** *Donor & government participation *Community development
1985+: Heroin use in hills 1987: Declaration of international conference calling for balanced approach	1980: Chicken curry with PM Kriangsak reconciliation	1988: Increased importance of demand reduction	**AD 3. 1990s Participatory Projects** *Donor, government & people participation Demand reduction
	1990s: NGOs in hills	1995+: Community-based treatment	
1998: UN recognizes threefold AD concept	1998: People's constitution		

IMPECT and a local group, the Mae Wang Watershed Network, is writing a book on Karen culture and history. The authors intend it to highlight the Karen way of life so that younger generations will take pride in their culture (*Khrongkan Phathana Laksut* 1997).

Interest in revitalizing tribal literature and cultural transmission from one generation to the next will, first of all, help projects meet the mandate of UN agencies. In addition, the local people, responding to the inherent value of such an approach, will participate to the point of taking the lead in their own development.

As the people begin to maintain and control information, alternative development work will become more successful. This is one important lesson gained from the Thai experience. With the active involvement of the people in their socio-economic development, the Thai model succeeds.

ACRONYMS

BMZ	Ministry of Economic Cooperation of the Federal Republic of Germany
CB-DAC	Community-Based Drug Abuse Control
CCDAC	Central Committee for Drug Abuse Control (Myanmar)
COHAN	Committee to Facilitate the Solution to National Security Problems Relating to Hilltribes and the Cultivation of Narcotics Crops
CRCDP	Crop Replacement and Community Development Project
CUSRI	Chulalongkorn University Social Research Institute
GPO	General Printing Office
GTZ	German Agency for Technical Cooperation
HAEP	Hill Areas Education Project
HAMP	Thai/United Nations Highland Agricultural Marketing and Production Project
HASD	Thai-Australia Highland Agricultural and Social Development Project
HDP	Highland Development Project
IMPECT	Inter-Mountain Peoples Education and Culture in Thailand Association
IO	India Office (London)
LCDC	Lao National Commission for Drug Control and Supervision
MOA	Ministry of Agriculture and Cooperatives
NESDB	National Economic and Social Development Board
NSO	National Statistics Office
ONCB	Office of Narcotics Control Board
PRA	Participatory Rural Appraisal

RDPB   Royal Development Projects Board
RFD   Royal Forest Department
TA-HASD   Thai-Australian Highland Agricultural and Social
             Development Project
TG-HDP   Thai-German Highland Development Programme
TN-HDP   Thai-Norwegian Church Aid Highland Development
             Project
UNFDAC   United Nations Fund for Drug Abuse Control
UNDCP   United Nations International Drug Control Programme
UNRISD   United Nations Research Institute for Social Development
USAID   United States Agency for International Development
USDA   United States Department of Agriculture

REFERENCES

UNITED NATIONS DOCUMENTS AND REPORTS

Anchalee Singhanetra-Renard. 1994. "Thailand's Illegal Drug Trade." Geneva: UNRISD (unpublished report).

Anek Nakabutara and Gary Suwannarat. 1994. "Community-Based Highland Drug Prevention and Treatment: Northern Thai Experiences, 1991–1994." Presented at the Seminar on Two Decades of Thai-UN Cooperation in Highland Development and Drug Control: Lessons Learned, Outstanding Issues, Future Directions; Chiang Mai.

Chaiwat Roongruangsee. 1994. "Development of Community Institution and Network: Village Organization in the Highland Development Process." Presented at the Seminar on Two Decades of Thai-UN Cooperation in Highland Development and Drug Control: Lessons Learned, Outstanding Issues, Future Directions; Chiang Mai.

Chayan Vaddhanaputi, et al. 1997. *Final Project Evaluation Report for "Strengthening Community-Based Drug Prevention Strategies in the Highlands of Northern Thailand" Project AD/THA/92/676*. Chiang Mai: Chiang Mai University Social Research Institute.

Commission of Enquiry into the Control of Opium-Smoking in the Far East. 1930. *Report to the Council*. Vol. 1. Geneva: League of Nations.

Crop Replacement and Community Development Project. 1973. "Progress Report—September 1972–June1973 [Chiang Mai]: mimeo.

Food and Agriculture Organization of the United Nations. 1978. *Mae Sa Integrated Watershed and Forest Land Use (Chiang Mai) Thailand Interim Report*. Rome: FAO. Because a second phase was expected, this Interim Report took the place of the Terminal Report that would normally be written at this stage of a project.

Francis, Paul et al. 1991. *Report of the Terminal In-Depth Evaluation Mission of Pae Por Highland Development Project.* N.p.: UNDCP.

HAMP [Thai/United Nations Highland Agricultural Marketing and Production Project]. 1979. *Highland Agricultural Marketing and Production Programme HAMPP A Joint UNFDAC/ONCP Project.* Chiang Mai.

Kanok Rerkasem. 1994. "Sustainable Agriculture." Presented at the Seminar on Two Decades of Thai-UN Cooperation in Highland Development and Drug Control: Lessons Learned, Outstanding Issues, Future Directions; Chiang Mai.

Mann, Richrd. 1984. *Terminal Report.* Chiang Mai: HAMP.

Moreland, Robert et al. 1993. "Evaluation of Assistance in Alternative Development in Thailand." Presented to UNDCP Bangkok.

Renard, Ronald D., et al. 1994. "Twenty Years of Highland Health and Education Development." Presented at the Seminar on Two Decades of Thai-UN Cooperation in Highland Development and Drug Control: Lessons Learned, Outstanding Issues, Future Directions; Chiang Mai.

Robert, G. Lamar and Ronald D. Renard. 1989. "Opium Crop Replacement without Tears or Terror: The Case of Northern Thailand 1971–1989." Prepared for the UNFDAC Regional Seminar on Replacement of Opium Poppy Cultivation; Swat, Pakistan.

Thai/UN Doi Yao Pha Mon HDP. 1989. *Project Document.* Bangkok: UNFDAC.

United Nations Consultative Group on Opium Problems. 1967. *Report.* New Delhi: Mimeograph (provisional report), no. GE 68-6080.

United Nations Development Programme. 1992. *Development Co-operation Thailand1990 Report.* Bangkok: UNDP.

United Nations Division of Narcotic Drugs. 1988. *Declaration of the International Conference on Drug Abuse and Illicit Trafficking and Comprehensive Multi-disciplinary Outline of Future Activities in Drug Abuse Control.* New York: United Nations.

United Nations Fund for Drug Abuse Control. 1975. *UN/Thai Programme for Drug Abuse Control in Thailand.* Geneva: UNFDAC. Progress Report 5 (January–June).

United Nations International Drug Control Progamme, 2000. *Thirty Years Fighting Drugs through Leadership and Participatory Cooperation:* UNDCP Regional Centre for East Asia and the Pacific.

United Nations International Drug Control Progamme Myanmar 2001. *The Drug Situation in the Union of Myanmar.* Yangon: UNDCP Country Office.

United Nations Preliminary Joint Survey Team. 1992. Reprinted as "Report of the Preliminary Joint Survey team on Opium Production and Consumption in the Union of Burma." *Thai-Yunnan Project Newsletter* 18, pp. 8–16. Canberra: Australian National University Research School of Pacific Studies. Originally published in 1964.

United Nations Survey Team. 1967. *Report of the United Nations Survey Team on the Economic and Social Needs of the Opium-Producing Areas in Thailand.* Bangkok: United Nations Survey Team.

Uraivan Tan-Kim-Yong et al. 1994. "Participatory Land Use Planning: A Method of Implementing Natural Resource Management." Presented at the Seminar on Two Decades of Thai-UN Cooperation in Highland Development and Drug Control: Lessons Learned, Outstanding Issues, Future Directions; Chiang Mai.

Williams, I.M.G. 1979. "UN/Thai programme for drug abuse control in Thailand—A Report on Phase I: February 1972–June 1979." *Bulletin on Narcotics* 31:2 (April–June), pp. 1–43.

Yingyos Chotpimai. 1987. "Third Army Area Narcotic Crops Cultivation Control Programme." In *Regional Seminar on Replacement of Opium Poppy Cultivation,* UNDP and UNFDAC. Chiang Mai: n.p.

THAI GOVERNMENT REPORTS AND DOCUMENTS

Aram Suwanbubpa. 1976. *Hill Tribe Development and Welfare Programmes in Northern Thailand.* Singapore: Regional Institute of Higher Education and Development.

COHAN. 1988. *Thamniap Ongkon Ekachon Thi Khao Ruam Prachum Sammana Ruang Kankaekhai Panha Chaokhao Lae Kamchat Kanpluk Phutseptit Phak Ekachon* [Directory of NGOs Attending the Seminar on Solving Hilltribe Problems and Controlling Narcotic Crop Production by the Private Sector]. Chiang Mai: COHAN.

———. 1990. *Sarupphon Kanprachumsammana Ruang Naeothang Kanchattham Phaen Phua Phathana Khunaphap Chiwit Khan Phunthan Chaokhao Phak Nua.* (Report of a Seminar on Guidelines for Drawing Up a Plan to Develop Basic Hilltribe Life in Northern Thailand). Chiang Mai: COHAN and Third Army Narcotics Crop Control Unit.

CUSRI et al. 1990. *Directory of Public Interest Non-Government Organizations in Thailand.* Bangkok: Chulalongkorn University.

Department of Public Welfare. 1962. *Report on the Socio-Economic Survey of the Hill Tribes in Northern Thailand.* Bangkok: Ministry of Interior.

―――. 1964. *A Brief on Hill Tribe Development and Welfare Program in Northern Thailand.* Bangkok: Ministry of Interior. In Thai and English.

Hill Area Education Project. 1986. *The Hill Areas Education Model: The 'Ashram' Approach to Community Education-Development.* Bangkok: PWD and Department of Non-formal Education.

Horticultural Crop Promotion Division. 1996. *Kaset Thisung Chak Adit Thung Patchuban* (Highland Agriculture from the Past to the Present). Bangkok: Ministry of Agriculture, Department of Agricultural Extension.

Kamon Ngamsomsuk and Narinchai Phathanaphongsa. 1996. *Rai-ngan Kansuksa Saphawa Thang Sethakit Lae Sangkhom Khong Kasetakon Nai Phunthi Khrongkan Luang 16 Haeng* (Report on the Study of Socio-Economic Conditions of Farmers in 16 Royal Project Sites). Bangkok: Highland Agriculture Division, Office of the Permanent Secretary of the Minister of Agriculture and Cooperatives.

Manndorff, Hans. 1969. *The Hill Tribe Program of the Public Welfare Department, Ministry of Interior, Thailand Research and Socio-economic Development.* Bangkok: Department of Public Welfare Division of Hill Tribe Welfare.

Ministry of National Development. 1970. *Ministry of National Development Handbook.* Bangkok: Ministry of National Development.

Munlanithi Khrongkan Luang [Royal Project]. 1995. Bangkok: The Royal Project.

NESDB. 1988. "The Second Masterplan for Highland Development and Narcotic Crops in Thailand." Bangkok: NESDB. Final draft.

NSO. 1976. *Report: Socio-Economic Survey 1975–76 Northern Region.* Bangkok: Office of the Prime Minister. In Thai and English.

ONCB. 1978–1997. *Thailand Narcotics Annual Reports.*

―――. 1983. *A Masterplan for Development of Opium Poppy Cultivating Regions of Thailand.* 2 vols. Bangkok: ONCB.

―――. 1994–2000. *Opium Cultivation and Eradication Report for Thailand: 1998–1999.* Bangkok: ONCB. In Thai until 1997, then in Thai and English.

————. 1995. *Ngan Khu Chiwit: Chawalit Yotmani* [Work is Life: Chavalit Yodmanee]. Bangkok: ONCB.

Royal Addresses and Speeches. 1970. Bangkok: Royal Household.

RPDB. 1997. *Concepts and Theories of His Majesty the King's Initiatives.* Bangkok: From Thai by the Royal Projects Development Board, translation sponsored by for UNDP and the Department of Technical and Economic Cooperation for presentation to His Majesty.

MONOGRAPHS, DISSERTATIONS, ARTICLES, AND OTHER OFFICIAL REPORTS

Alting Von Geusau, Leo. 1983. "Dialectics of Akha Zang: The Interiorisations of a Perennial Minority Group." In *Highlanders of Thailand,* edited by John McKinnon and Wanat Bhruksasri, pp. 243–277. Kuala Lumpur: Oxford.

Anusorn Kunanusorn et al. 1986. *Thailand Vegetable Marketing Project Phase I: Fresh and Processed Vegetable Market Survey.* Chiang Mai: Payap University Research Center Publication No. 12.

Aran Suwanbubpa. 1976. *Hill Tribe Development and Welfare Programmes in Northern Thailand.* Singapore: Regional Institute of Higher Education and Development.

Bernatzik, Hugo Otto. 1947. *Akha und Meau.* Innsbruck: Wagner'sche Univ. Buchdrukerei.

BMZ and GTZ. 1983. *Thai-German Highland Development Programme: Evaluation Report.* Bonn: BMZ and GTZ.

Brandenberg, Leo. 1985. *Thai-German Highland Development Programme: A Concept for A Regional Rural Development Project.* Rev. ed. Chiang Mai: Thai-German Highland Development Programme Internal Paper 3.

CB-DAC Core Team. 1997. *Review of the Implementation of Community-Based Drug Abuse Control.* Chiang Mai: TG-HDP Internal Paper No. 204.

Chambers, Robert. 1992. "Rapid but relaxed and participatory rural appraisal: towards applications in health and nutrition. In *Rapid Assessment Procedures: Qualitative Methodologies for Planning and Evaluation of Health Related Programmes,* edited by N. S. Scrimshaw and G. R. Gleason, pp. 295–305. Boston: International Nutrition Foundation for Developing Countries.

————. Robert. 1997. *Whose Reality Counts?.* London: Intermediate Technology Development Group.

Chanthana Fong-thale. 1993. *Chak Doi Yao Thung Phu Phachi* [From Doi Yao to Phu Phachi]. Bangkok: Chap Kra.

Chatchai Ratanakeere. 1998. "A Community and Narcotics." In *From Ideas . . . to Action: Experiences in Participatory Highland Development,* edited by Naret et al., pp. 65–68. Chiang Mai: TG-HDP Internal Paper No. 211.

Chatchawan Thongdiloet. 2001. "Green Movement or Green Party: Different Strategies to Promote the Green Agenda in Thailand." Presentation at the meeting of the Heinrich Böll Foundation being edited for publication. Chiang Mai: Heinrich Böll Foundation.

Chayan Vaddhanaphuti. 1986. *Thai-German Highland Development Programme Social Sector Evaluation Report.* Chiang Mai: TG-HDP.

di Gennaro, Giuseppe. 1991. *La guerra della droga.* Rome: Mondadori.

Enters, Thomas. 1992. "Land Degradation and Resource Conservation in the Highlands of Northern Thailand—the Limits to Economic Evaluations." Ph.D. diss., Australian National University, Canberra.

Geddes, William Robert. 1976. *Migrants of the Mountains: The Cultural Ecology of the Blue Miao (Hmong Njua) of Thailand.* Oxford: Clarendon.

Hoare, Peter. *Methodology of Rural Development in Northern Thailand.* Chiang Mai, n.p.

Ingram, James C. 1971. *Economic Change in Thailand 1850–1970.* Kuala Lumpur: Oxford.

IO. L/PandS/60 "Elias to Viscount," 15 February 1890, pp. 1104–1106 (Enclosures #3 and #4).

Kampe, Ken. 1989. *Reviewing Mae Chaem: The Past, Present and Future of the Mae Chaem Watershed Development Project.* Chiang Mai: n.p.

————. 1992. "Northern Highlands Development, Bureaucracy and Life on the Margins." *Pacific Viewpoint* 33:2, pp. 159–164.

Keen, F.G. 1984. "End of Contract Report." Chiang Mai: typescript.

Khanitha Lekhakun et al., eds. 1996. *Praphatton Bon Doi* [Royal Travels in the Hills]. Bangkok: Royal Project.

Khanitha Lekhakun, ed. *Doi Tung.* 1998. Bangkok: Tourist Authority of Thailand. In Thai.

Khrongkan Phathana Laksut Thongthin Nai Radap Prathom Suksa Chon Phao Pwakeryaw [Project to Draw Up a Primary School Curriculum on the Karen People]. Chiang Mai: Mae Wang Watershed Community Network, Chiang Mai Provincial Primary Education Headquarters et al. n.d. ca. 1997.

Kingshill, Konrad. 1991. *Ku Daeng—Thirty Years Later: A Village Study in Northern Thailand 1954–1984.* DeKalb: Northern Illinois University Center for Southeast Asian Studies Monograph Series on Southast Asia Special Report No. 26.

Klein, Otome Hutheesing. 1990. *Emerging Sexual Inequality Among the Lisu of Northern Thailand.* Leiden: Brill.

Krogh, Jr. Egil. n.d. Online interview at http://www.pbs.org/wgbh/pages/frontline/shows/drugs/interviews/krogh.html

Lao National Commission for Drug Control and Supervision. 1993. *Proposal for a Comprehensive Drug Control Programme.* 4 vols. Vientiane: LCDC.

Lee, Gar Yia. 1981. "The Effects of Development Measures on the Socio-Economy of the White Hmong." Ph.D. diss.,. University of Sydney.

Lewis, Paul. 1985. "Effects of Opium on Tribal People in Thailand." Mimeo.

McCoy, Alfred W. 1991. *The Politics of Heroin: CIA Complicity in the Global Drug Trade.* Chicago: Lawrence Hill.

Mann, Richard S. 1994. *Final Report: Baw Gaow Phase IV/Cham Luang Phase II Tribal Detoxification and Rehabilitation Project.* Baw Gaow, Chiang Mai: typescript.

Miles, Douglas. 1974. "Marriage, Agriculture and Ancestor Worship among the Pulangka Yao." Ph.D. diss., University of Sydney.

Myanmar CCDAC. 1991. "Supply and Demand Reduction in the Union of Myanmar." Paper presented at the Meeting of Senior Officials on Drug Abuse Issues in Asia and the Pacific, Tokyo, 13–15 February.

Naret Songkrawsook et al., eds. 1998. *From Ideas . . . to Action: Experiences in Participatory Highland Development.* Chiang Mai: TG-HDP Internal Paper No. 211.

Owen, David Edward. 1934. *British Opium Policy in China and India.* New Haven: Yale.

Pairote Pornjongman and Orapin Wimonpusit. 1998. "Learning . . . Coordinating . . . Rehabilitating." In *From Ideas . . . to Action: Experiences in Participatory Highland Development,* edited by Naret et al. Chiang Mai: TG-HDP Internal Paper No. 211.

Pasuk Phongpaichit and Chris Baker. 1998. *Thailand's Boom and Bust.* Chiang Mai: Silkworm Books.

Pornthep Iamprapai. 1999. "Highland Development Experiences in Thailand." Paper presented at the China/Myanmar Alternative

Development Cooperation Meeting, Simao, Yunnan, China, 6–9 April.

Radley, Howard. 1986. "Economic Marginalization and the Ethnic Consciousness of the Green Mong (Moob Ntsuab) of Northwestern Thailand," Ph.D. diss., Oxford University.

Renard, Ronald D. 1994. "The Monk, the Hmong, the Forest, the Cabbage, Fire and Water: Incongruities in Northern Thailand Opium Replacement." *Law and Society Review* 28:3, pp. 657–664.

———. 1996. *The Burmese Connection: Illegal Drugs and the Making of the Golden Triangle.* Boulder: Lynne Rienner.

———. 2001. "On the Possibility of Early Karen Settlement in the Chiang Mai Valley." Paper presented at The International Workshop on Inter-Ethnic Relations in the Making of Mainland Southeast Asia and Southwestern China, sponsored by Kyoto University Center for Southeast Asian Studies, Chiang Rai, March.

Research Review Team. 1977. *Thai/ARS Crop Substitution Program.* Beltsville: USDA Agricultural Research Service.

Roth, Alan D., et al. 1983. *Evaluation of the Mae Chaem Watershed Development Project.* Washington D.C.: Development Alternatives, Inc.

Sen, Amartya. 1999. *Development as Freedom.* New York: Knopf.

Supaporn Jarunpattana. 1980. "Phasi Fin Kap Naiyobai Kankhlang Khong Rathaban Ph.S. 2367–2468 (Opium Revenue and Fiscal Policy of Thailand 1824–1925)." Master's thesis, Chulalongkorn University, Bangkok.

Tapp, Nicholas. 1989. *Sovereignty and Rebellion: The White Hmong of Northern Thailand.* Oxford: Oxford University Press.

Thai-Australia Highland Agricultural and Social Development Project. 1987. *Project Brief.* Chiang Mai: Australian Agricultural Consulting and Management Company.

Tuanchai Dithet. 1985. *Mae Chan: Sai Nam Thi Phanplian* [Mae Chan: A River of Change]. Bangkok: Thianwan.

USAID. 1980. *Project Paper: Thailand-Hill Areas Education 493-0297.* Bangkok: USAID Thailand.

U.S. Congress. House of Representatives Committee on International Relations. 1975. *Proposal to Control Opium for the Golden Triangle and Terminate the Shan Opium Trade.* 94th Cong., 1st sess. Washington, D.C.: GPO.

U.S. Department of State, Bureau of International Narcotics Matters. 1992. *1991 International Narcotics Control Strategy Report.* Washington, D.C.: GPO.

Vibhavadi Rangsit, Princess. 1997. *"Mua Nua Phraratchathan Khun Khao"* [When the Royal Assistance Unit Went Up the Hills]. In *Anuson 20 Pi Vibhavadi Rangsit* [Twenty Year Memorial of Vibhavadi Rangsit], pp. 64–81. Bangkok.

———. 1970. *Sadet Doi* (Visiting the Hills). A Daily Record of a Stay at Bhubhing Palace in Chiang Mai. Published in cremation volume for Thao Wanida Phicharini (Bang Sanitwong Na Ayutthaya), 30 March 1970. Bangkok.

"The Wonderland of Opium." 1971. *Far Eastern Economic Review* (July 24), p. 37.

USAID/Thailand. 1980. *Project Paper: Thailand–Mae Chaem Watershed Development Project.* Bangkok: USAID.

Westermeyer, Joseph. 1982. *Poppies, Pipes, and People: Opium and its Use in Laos.* Berkeley: University of California.

Worcester, Dean C. 1913. "The Non-Christian Peoples of the Philippine Islands." *The National Geographic Magazine* 24:11, pp. 1157–1256.

Zhou Yongming. 1999. *Anti-Drug Crusades in Twentieth-Century: Nationalism, History and State Building.* Lanham: Rowman and Littlefield.

Zinke, Paul J., et al. 1978. "Soil Fertility Aspects of the Lua' Forest Fallow System of Shifting Cultivation." In *Farmers in the Forest,* edited by Peter Kunstadter et al, pp. 134–159. Honolulu: East-West Center.

PERSONAL COMMUNICATIONS

1997
Wanat Bhruksasri; former Director, Tribal Research Institute, Chiang Mai

2000
Dr. Sanong Chinnanon; Alternative Development Cooperation Project Coordinator, UNDCP Regional Centre, Bangkok

Mr. Bengt Juhlin; Senior Programme Coordinator, UNDCP Regional Centre, Bangkok

Dr. Sandro Calvani; Representative, UNDCP Regional Centre, Bangkok

Mr. Steven Carson; former Director, Thai-UN Integrated Pockets Area Development Project

Mr. Prasong Jantakard; former Community-Based Project Officer, Thai-German Highland Development Programme

Akha and Lahu leaders and elders; DAPA organization (Development Agriculture and Education Project for Akha), Chiang Rai

Dr. Ken Kampe; former Senior Advisor, Mae Chaem Integrated Watershed Development Project (USAID-funded); former consultant to Thai-German Highland Development Programme and other projects, Chiang Mai (several meetings)

Dr. Charles Kaplan; University of Maastricht, Netherlands

Mr. Phonthep Iamprapha; former Director, Thai-UN Doi Yao-Pha Mon Highland Development Project, Chiang Rai

Dr. Charles Mehl; Assistant Director, Mae Fah Luang Foundation, Bangkok

Police General Prasong Sisombun; Deputy Director, Doi Tung Development Project

Mr. Narong Phothiphaichot; Director, Training Center, Doi Tung Development Project

Mr. Narong Aphichai; Manager, Coffee and Macadamia Nut Processing Factory, Doi Tung Development Project

Mr. Suchin Tophangthian; Manager, Vetiver Grass Center, Doi Tung Development Project

Mr. Thamnu Sirisingha; Director, ONCB Northern Regional Office

Mr. Mathee Wongpradit; Director, Intelligence Division, ONCB Northern Regional Office

Mr. Yotsapong Kukaewkasem; Director, Development Agriculture and Agriculture Project for Akha (DAPA)

Mr. Luka Chermui; Akha leader and Director, Akha Medical Clinic

Dr. Halvor Kolshus; UNDCP Country Representative for Lao PDR.

Mr. Pititham Thitimontre; District Officer, Si Chiang Mai, Nong Khai province (former Director, Thai-German Highland Development Programme, 1989).

Mr. Mongkol Chandraprasert; Tribal Research Institute, Chiang Mai

Mr. Beno; former Headman, Doi Chang Village, Mae Suai district, Chiang Mai.

Mr. Yotsapong Kaewkukasem; Director, DAPA, Chiang Rai

Mr. Tanupong Deetet; Public Welfare Department, Phayao province

Mr. Samphan; head, Public Welfare Department Office, Phayao province

Yao elders; Pang Kha (Pulangka) village, Phayao province

Mr. Pipop Chamnivikaipong; Director of Survey and Report Unit, ONCB, Chiang Mai

Mr. Banlu; Engineer, Highway Department, Chiang Mai

Mr. Suthat Pleumpanya; Director, Highland Agricultural Development Division (former office manager, Royal Project)

Mr. Hagen Dirksen; former Senior Advisor, Thai-German Highland Development Programme

Police General Chavalit Yodmani; former Secretary General, ONCB 1983–1995.

Mr. Narong Suwanapiam; on staff of HAMP and other projects; later ONCB Deputy Secretary General

Mr. Kamol Thaiyapirom; on staff of HAMP and other projects, now in ONCB Northern Regional Headquarters

Dr. Horleifur Jonsson; anthropologist, Arizona State University; doctoral dissertation research on Yao/Mien in Phayao

Mr. Richard L. Mann; American Baptist missionary in Thailand since 1959; on staff, usually as senior adviser for several UNFDAC/ UNDCP highland development projects from 1971 until 1990.

Dr. John McKinnon; geographer, Advisor to Tribal Research Centre/ Institute in mid 1970s and mid 1980s; conducted research on Doi Chang in 1980s.

Dr. Kirsten Ewer, researcher of Karens in Huai Kha Khaeng, Uthai Thani

INDEX